White Weddings an
by
E. Mulholl

COPYRIGHT

Text copyright © 2016 **E. Mulholland**
All Rights Reserved

The right of **Ellen Jamison**, writing under the pseudonym **E. Mulholland**, to be identified as the Author of the Work has been asserted in accordance with Copyright, Designs and Patents Act 1988.

No part of this publication may be reproduced, stored or transmitted in any form or by any means without the prior consent of the author.

All characters in this publication are entirely fictional and any resemblance to real persons, living or dead, is purely coincidental.

ABOUT THE AUTHOR

E. Mulholland was bitten by the writing bug at a very young age. Now in her twenties, she is a prolific author who loves to create stories that will excite and enthral readers. She lives in England.

DEDICATION

To my family for their love and support

PROLOGUE

Valentine's Day

Charlotte

Charlotte dumped her bags at the door, hung her keys over the hook, sunk her aching feet into fluffy slippers and let her senses feast on the rich aroma filtering from the country-style kitchen.

'Mmm, smells delicious,' she wrapped her arms around the man seasoning two beef fillets with black pepper, garlic and rosemary.

Sautéing shallots, John added a dash of velvety port.

'Very fancy,' she smiled, examining the beverage before it was rehomed in the lattice rack.

'Well, it is Valentine's Day.'

'Yes, but it's our sixth as a couple and you've never once splurged on wine.'

For hopeless romantics like Charlotte, every February 14th was a cause for celebration. Relationship status was irrelevant. Even as a singleton, she had savoured the day when love conquered hate and happily curled up with a giant teddy who sang one chorus of *Love Is All Around* if she remembered to put batteries in his backside or she'd festooned her mantelpiece with Valentine's cards, not caring if the insides were blank, watched soppy films and added bits and bobs to the scrapbook of ideas she'd been gathering for her perfect wedding since her school days.

'What makes this year so significant?' she questioned.

'Nothing,' he said, shrugging, though his nonchalance was far from convincing.

It piqued Charlotte's concern. So did his body language. John was a rare species of male who didn't treat the kitchen like dangerous territory, but now she noticed beads of sweat, fidgeting footwork, a jittery grasp of the frying pan that seared the fillets.

'Phew, it's hot in here,' he shoved open the window. 'Must be a mild night.'

In reality, Mother Nature had acted cruelly this month. She exhaled bitterly cold air that numbed body parts, turned pavements into treacherous strips of black ice, cackling mercilessly as pedestrians tripped and tumbled, buried the landscape under a slab of snow so thick that commuters had to chisel a path to work and paralysed plants. Now she directed a draught into the nooks and crannies of Charlotte's apricot cardigan. To thaw out, she perched on the iron radiator. Not wise.

'John, if you feel feverish,' Charlotte said, fanning her burnt bum with a dishcloth, 'we can postpone dinner. Maybe you're coming down with flu.'

'No, I'm fine. Too many cups of coffee between lectures. Don't worry.'

Both foodies, the kitchen was the heart of their home. Cooking apple green walls were harmonious with rustic units, shelves were lined with Mason jars and Pestle & Mortar bowls and a chalkboard shaped like a cow was sketched with diary dates. Handwritten recipes and aphorism plaques – *Meals and Memories Made Here* – added quirkiness.

'Did you take the test?' John asked, gulping the entire contents of a glass of tap water in one mouthful.

'Um, no...' she scrambled a list of excuses. 'Two teachers were off sick and there was a scuffle in the playground and I had a mountain of homework to mark.'

The grim truth was Charlotte had done the deed. Locked in the staff toilets, tears magnified the blue line indicating another negative result. *Not pregnant.* But honesty would have to wait. She forbade the news from ruining her favourite day of the year.

'I'll lay the table,' she said, switching the focus before they were pricked by this thorny subject.

Situated in a rural Cheshire village, twists of ivy decorated the original sash windows of their small cottage with a garden that tumbled down to meet the stream meandering through the patchwork of fields and farmland. She loved the cottage's period features, wooden beams and exposed brickwork, the fact each room had a past, a story to tell. The sense that she and John were custodians of a piece of history sown into the fabric of this community.

Charlotte festooned its interior with prints and patterns inspired by the cottage garden that she curated. The dining room was no exception. Bluebells, daisies and lilacs stencilled the wallpaper, ashwood furniture made by local carpenters exuded quaint charm and a shaggy cream rug warmed the exposed floorboards. Above the inglenook fireplace, heart-shaped picture frames showcased a montage of happy memories.

'Great choice,' John called, sarcastically, as she selected a CD of love songs.

The past six years of coupledom had shown Charlotte that his hard shell protected a gooey centre.

'Glad you approve,' she teased, turning up the volume.

She swooned to *The Way You Look Tonight* while unfurling the shimmering gold table runner and layering plates and bowls. A dozen red roses, a gift from him to her, formed Cupid's centrepiece. She tied red, pink and purple foil balloons to the chairs, arranged beaded flower napkin rings and lit a scented candle that bathed the room in a soft yellow glow.

Inhaling its infusion of bergamot, chocolate and patchouli, Charlotte tied up loose strands from her endearingly chaotic nest of strawberry blonde curls and scattered red heart confetti over the table.

•

The oysters were heaven in half a shell.

'Best of all,' John spoke while he shucked. 'They boost fertility.'

Guilt-ridden, Charlotte identified a diversion.

'Happy Valentine's Day, darling,' she produced his gift in bounteous folds of themed wrapping paper.

John admired the brown leather wallet. Twenty years Charlotte's senior, he was a debonair 52-year-old university professor of history who wore his age with pride. He didn't try to emulate modern men. Grunge fashion was an alien concept and he commanded respect in classic tailoring.

'Thank you,' he rewarded Charlotte with a kiss.

Fingers like pincers, she hovered over the strawberry champagne truffles on the sideboard while he served their main course.

'Don't spoil your appetite,' he playfully slapped her thieving hand.

It wasn't possible to stay angry at Charlotte. She had a plump face full of character – kindly brown eyes, freckles, a button nose, dimples and a lopsided mouth always flecked up into a smile. Like a mother hen, children flocked to her. Everybody loved Charlotte. She spoke as if each word was a song.

'Wow,' Charlotte exclaimed, carving the tender meat. 'John, the starter was scrumptious, but you've improved upon perfection.'

She reached for the bottle of wine.

'Haven't you had enough?' John raised his eyebrows. 'Better safe than sorry if the test turns out to be positive.'

'Oh, um, just a habit.'

The telephone rang. She was saved by the proverbial bell. At the end of the line, Charlotte discerned his daughter's squeaky 9-year-old voice. Inadvertently fathering a child from a brief first marriage, she presumed John would not countenance kids with her, but she had to reconsider when he hinted that she shouldn't get a repeat prescription for the pill.

They had been trying to conceive for a year. Unlike John, their struggle was not shrouded in mystery for Charlotte. She had an inhospitable womb. Expecting to grow a child in her uterus was like expecting a delicate flower to thrive in a nuclear wasteground. But, a decade on from the diagnosis, Charlotte still wasn't reconciled to a life without kids. Everyone at school said she was like Mary Poppins – a natural with children – and she chose not to remind them the character had none of her own. Infertility was particularly cruel for a homemaker, a woman who wished she could adopt her nieces and nephews, a primary-school teacher whose day job was devoted to under-11s and one who couldn't look at a baby without aching ovaries.

'Chloe sounds excitable,' she commented, fawning over the wilted spinach as he returned to the opposite chair.

'She got her first Valentine's card.'

'Ooh, from a secret admirer?'

'Not exactly. He's a boy that she's liked since nursery. It was hidden in her biology textbook on the *Anatomy of the Human Heart* page.'

'Aww,' Charlotte cooed over the budding couple.

A protective dad, John's smile was a sceptical slit. It reconfirmed how brilliant a parent he would be for a baby of their own.

'She's only nine,' he groaned.

'You're never too young to fall in love.'

'In other news,' he dismissed the corniness. 'Chloe's following in your footsteps.'

'She wants to be a teacher?'

'No, a Girl Guide. The school reckons that she demonstrates the "commitment, compassion and competency" the organisation values.'

'All good attributes for a Guider.'

'And for an older sister.'

'Hmm...'

The oven timer pinged. John disappeared to fetch dessert. It felt like she'd been given a second stay of execution.

'Ladies first,' he handed Charlotte the knife.

Drooling, she sliced the warm chocolate gateau, but the blade hit a solid object. Charlotte separated the slices to take a closer look at the shiny metal band while John knelt on the carpet. Only then did she realise why he was so nervous.

'Charlotte,' he asked, 'will you marry me?'

Titania

If Paris was a person, Titania would have made love to it. Crowned the world's most romantic destination, the capital city had captured her heart like no man ever could. Their relationship was a whirlwind. Love-at-first-sight. She was currently spellbound by a moonlit view of this cauldron of culture as it simmered under the sky full of stars.

'Arc de Triomphe,' her boyfriend pointed, flaunting his perfect pronunciation in a language that disguised his normal plummy voice.

Steeped in history, the arch juxtaposed the Louvre's modern glass pyramid where the posh couple had marvelled at the *Mona Lisa*. Following his finger, she saw the Champs-Elysées. The famous boulevard was a hive of late-night activity. Fashionistas impervious to the frosty temperatures channelled Coco Chanel in candy pink suits with braided trims or LBDs layered with strands of pearls and sashayed out of boutiques with a designer purchase tucked neatly in their quilted purse. Scholars headed to the theatre. A French family of gourmands sampled the finest haute cuisine at a Michelin-starred restaurant.

'Gosh, it's so pretty,' Titty admired the boats bobbing gently on the Seine.

Nature's divide, the river cut the city into two distinct halves. The eclectic Left Bank, a haven for writers and artists, its smoky bars now populated with students from the Sorbonne debating the genius of Camus or Maupassant. Roderick and Titty preferred the Right Bank. Traditionally the epicentre of French politics, finance and commerce, it was an affluent area inhabited by professionals like them who exuded suave sophistication.

'La pièce de résistance,' Roderick concluded the tour. 'C'est Notre-Dame.'

The cathedral had a gothic silhouette, jagged turrets spiking the sky, but the most imposing landmark was their present location. Illuminated by golden beams, the Eiffel Tower was an architectural masterpiece, a structure worthy of its icon status.

To honour Valentine's Day, Cupid had revamped the champagne bar on the observatory deck. Heart bunting, fairy lights, red macaroons for *messieurs* and white marshmallows for *madames* had lured hordes of tourists to toast their love at the top of the tower. Many gravitated towards the chocolate fountain installed below the bottles on the curved counter. The drinks menu had not escaped the Roman god of love's redecoration with dark, sexy and mysterious cocktails like *Devil Woman*, flirty liqueurs garnished with a provocatively plump cherry and traditional wines poured into pink sugar-encrusted glasses.

'Happy Valentine's Day,' Roderick proffered a flute of rosé.

'You, too.'

'Has Paris met your expectations?'

'Exceeded them.'

Kissing, they clinked glasses.

'Brrr,' Titty reacted to the chilly breeze.

Dressed for dinner at The Ritz, she had only a bolero over her beaded column gown.

'I told you to bring a coat,' Roderick admonished.

'I didn't have space in my suitcase.'

'Packing is an art you're yet to master.'

'You're right.'

'Aren't I always?'

'Yes, darling, you are.'

With a puff of haughty self-righteousness, Roderick draped his suit jacket around her shivering shoulders, the 18ct yellow gold signet ring on his pinkie catching the light. The silk lining of the Italian wool garment soothed Titty's prickly rash of goose-pimples.

'Ooh la la,' the bartender applauded the pair, 'un couple parfait.'

Despite floundering in French, Titty got the gist. Tall, dark, and handsome, both had won the genetic jackpot. Evoking comparisons to the thoroughbreds at her family's stables, Titty had equine features, a mane of glossy chestnut locks slung over one shoulder in a plait and tied with a red ribbon as if primed for a dressage competition and she was blessed with the long limbs and graceful gait of a prize racehorse. The lord was an oil painting waiting to happen.

Roderick, she agreed with the bartender, was pretty much perfect. And he was a superhero barrister. He prosecuted war criminals, mass murderers and genocidal maniacs during the week and spent his spare hours competing in charity triathlons, teaching underprivileged schoolkids a foreign language, thrashing the opposition at squash or polo, mastering fiendish Sudoku. Yes, he was arrogant, but nobody could deny the old-Etonian had plenty of reasons to brim with conceited confidence.

So surely Titty was right to ignore the fact she'd been more seduced by Paris than by him during their relationship that had spanned a whole ten years?

•

The shrill ringtone of Titty's mobile interrupted Roderick's analysis of the French Revolution.

'Sorry, it's work,' she explained, hurriedly swallowing a marshmallow.

'Take the call.'

'No, it's inconvenient, I'll direct Dr Monaghan to a different doctor.'

'And let a rival get the credit for helping?'

'Okay,' Titty was persuaded, 'but I won't be long.'

'Don't hurry back.'

Roderick never begrudged the crazy schedule of a cardiothoracic registrar even if it meant their lives diverged for days, weeks or months. In fact, he was the engine of her driving ambition, revving her up if she felt down, patching over any puncture with a rousing pep talk and keeping her foot glued to the throttle with grand promises when she made it to the top tier of medicine.

'Prescribe beta-blockers,' Titty advised her junior, 'and complete hourly observations.'

Like the strongest dose of Valium, her cool competence calmed Dr Monaghan's nerves. Afterwards, Titty rang the ICU ward for an update on Oliver, if there was evidence of any improvement. The nurse's silence was deafening. Like the ear-splitting siren of the ambulance that first rushed her brother to hospital. The sound that still haunted her.

'Oliver loved French at school,' she reminisced, peering over the balustrade at the Trocadéro gardens where people posed for photos backdropped by twenty water cannons in the Warsaw fountains. 'I must take a copy of *Le Monde* onto the ward and read it to him.'

'Why bother?' Roderick scorned. 'He can't bloody hear you. The poor bugger's in a coma.'

'No, he's in a persistent vegetative state.'

'Same difference.'

'No, it's not.'

'It'd be like reading to a zombie.'

'No, an abundance of case studies suggest patients with brain injuries can register voices,' she insisted.

'Emphasis on *suggest*.'

'Oliver can hear me,' she was adamant. 'He knows I'm there. He can sense my presence.'

'Titty, darling, you're deluded.'

But, averse to conflict, Roderick used flattery to soothe the scars inflicted on her sensitive skin. It was a tried-and-tested technique. For Titty, praise equalled pleasure.

'You'd be a strong candidate for the consultant post,' he arrested her attention.

'You really believe I stand a chance?' Titty spluttered on her rosé.

'Absolutely, provided you work hard and accept your father's offer to bribe the board of governors.'

'You know I'm uncomfortable with cheating.'

'It's not cheating,' Roderick silenced her doubts with the assertiveness he used to win arguments in court, 'it's commitment to the cause.'

'Yes, darling.'

'Good girl.'

Back in his good books, Titty relaxed, but not for long.

'Although,' he admonished, 'the promotion would have been far more impressive if achieved before your 30th birthday.'

Titty was flabbergasted.

'That's incredibly tough. Most consultants have accumulated decades of experience. I only qualified as a doctor five years ago.'

'Tough,' he conceded, swilling his wine like a true connoisseur, an action that made every woman in the vicinity swoon, 'but not impossible.'

Roderick's support was a thin mask for pressure. Compliments were back-handed. Her successes were never sufficient. If this was a school report, *must try harder* would be the patronising feedback, but Titty kept trying, desperate to be the teacher's pet.

'If you want to be the best,' he lectured, 'you have to push boundaries, set new records.'

As usual, his tone planted seeds of doubt that spread faster than a mile-a-minute Russian vine. It strangled any shoots of self-esteem.

'You're right,' Titty agreed, struck by a familiar pang of shame. 'Maybe I got complacent.'

Although she didn't know how, given her mind never strayed from medicine. They were surgically attached. Pardon the pun.

'Hopefully you won't let me down this year.'

'Roderick, that's never my intention.'

'But it's often the reality.'

Titty's eyes burned with humiliated tears that she refused to shed in public.

'If you get the job,' he pursed his lips, 'your workload is bound to increase so we shouldn't delay wedding preparations.'

Absorbed in the city, Roderick's final words shocked her. He had plotted the future of their relationship when their paths first crossed as students. A laminated copy of the document was magnetised to their fridge like a legal precedent that could not be changed and Titty knew a proposal was forecast to coincide with their tenth anniversary. But the specifics were a surprise.

On one knee, her boyfriend revealed a ring with a diamond that rivalled the colour and clarity of the stars studding the night sky.

'Titania,' he asked, 'will you marry me?'

Zoë

'Faster!' Zoë yelled, the syllables almost stolen by the whooshing wind.

Fuelled by Dutch courage, her boyfriend obeyed her need for speed. Doing double the limit had got her adrenalin pumping. But it didn't satiate her appetite for acceleration.

'Crank it up! Don't be shy! Put your foot to the floor!'

Josh moved into top gear.

'You're such a dare devil,' he screamed, as his customised convertible that cost double the average house price raced along the road.

'It's not fun unless it's forbidden!' Zoë tantalised him with the innuendo.

Too rural for streetlamps, the country lane that Josh was navigating like a Formula One race course was enveloped by darkness. They blindly hit a hairpin bend. The sporty alloy wheels screeched, tyres zigzagging the tarmac. Trapped in a vortex of velocity, Zoë's face was lashed by her peroxide blonde extensions as they spun madly before hurtling to a standstill.

Alcohol had demolished all traces of fear. Like a pair of silly schoolkids on a joy ride, the convertible shook with their claps and cheers at the death-defying manoeuvre.

'Woah,' Josh exclaimed, hands still gripping the steering wheel.

'That was so awesome.'

'Yeah.'

'Let's do it again.'

'You bet.'

Josh reversed out of the ditch without checking his mirrors. A tractor tooted, its driver making an emergency brake as his panicked expression was caught in the beam of their headlamps. They didn't care. Zoë turned on the radio. Club bangers blasted from the speakers and they shouted the lyrics until hoarse.

•

Rockingham Palace was a crash course in tasteless extravagance. And Zoë loved every square inch. Crunching the gravel driveway, Josh parked outside his mock Tudor mansion in an exclusive cul-de-sac in Alderley Edge, Cheshire that was illuminated by sensory lights.

'We broke the speed-o-meter,' he laughed, switching off the ignition with the press of a button.

Once a cheetah, the engine quietened to the purr of a domesticated cat.

'I know,' she slurred, 'we could've been arrested.'

'Or had a serious accident.'

'Life-changing injuries…'

'Or worse.'

The sobering prospect momentarily curbed their enthusiasm.

'But I don't regret a second,' he whispered, intoxicating her with his pungent cologne as he leant closer for a snog.

'Me, neither.'

Roaring with laughter, they stayed seated while their galloping heart rates returned to normal.

'I can't believe what happened in the restaurant,' Zoë said, removing her mobile from the glove box where she'd snapped the photographic evidence.

'Yeah,' Josh agreed, 'but who can blame the guy for fainting? The tip I left was more than he made a month.'

'You're so generous.'

'Well, it's Valentine's Day, time to spread the love.'

'Ha-ha.'

During their romantic dinner, Zoë had snapped the waiter's severe shock. The cash bonus made him fall the floor where he remained, spread-eagled, until revived by smelling salts courtesy of the chef. His disbelief wasn't unlike hers. Hobnobbing with the country's highest earners was still a novelty given that she'd only been dating the footballer for six weeks, less time than it took for her to squeeze into the Spanx keeping her lumps and bumps at bay. Although she suspected her reaction at Josh's weekly pay cheques would never grow old. Like the skin of the Botoxed brigade of celebrities, it would be forever young.

'You were brave to try fish eggs,' he said.

'Fish eggs?'

'Yeah, you know, the main ingredient of caviar. The £250 dish you ordered. It's amazing what restaurants charge for black goop.'

The grim reality made her stomach churn. More accustomed to cabbage than Beluga caviar, Zoë had no idea what it constituted. Now she was on the verge of vomiting over his convertible's white leather upholstery as she envisaged salt-cured roe swimming up her intestines.

'Well, it's a delicacy,' she lied to conceal her ignorance. 'The best caviar I've eaten.'

'A delicacy?' he wasn't convinced. 'It's more like a bushtucker trial on *I'm a Celebrity Get Me out Of Here*.'

The high-octane entertainment had left Zoë windswept. While Josh grabbed his bomber jacket from the rear seat, she heaped a top coat of make-up onto her piggish features, scooping out masses of product from her pots and potions with hands like shovels. All garish pinks and neon yellows.

'I expected more paparazzi at the restaurant,' she commented, sliding off the seat.

Although Zoë was an adrenalin-junkie, it was a mighty relief to get out of the car. Dinner had strained her bejewelled bandage dress which exposed every inch of fake-tanned flesh. Standing reduced the pressure on her rib cage and she took her first proper breath for an hour.

'*Le Mouton* is very upmarket,' he said, 'so the privacy policy is super strict.'

'Oh, of course.'

'Nice to dine in peace, though, wasn't it?'

'Yep.'

The casual tone was another lie. Zoë didn't suffer shyness – the gene was absent from her chromosomal make-up – and had engineered numerous opportunities to land a spot in a celebrity magazine. All to no avail. But, if she kept pretending to be a girlfriend not a gold-digger, she hoped to soon get a double-page wedding spread.

'Thank you for a wonderful night,' she gushed, latching onto his arm as they drunkenly stumbled to the pillared entrance.

Ooh, Zoë flinched, excited by the bulge of his bicep. Not even the coarsest Brillo pad could scrub off her smile from snaring football's most eligible bachelor. Outwitting the bouncers, she had invaded a New Year bash at a nightclub popular with rich and famous sports stars. Her latex playsuit and stripper shoes guaranteed a second glance.

Josh wasn't just a footballer; he was a premier league footballer. His weekly salary eclipsed what Zoë's fashion boutique generated a year. But his bank balance wasn't the only lure. Fit and fashionable, he rocked a crew cut and diamond earrings and was a walking advertisement for the male grooming products he endorsed on billboards up and down the country. Zoë couldn't resist a man who moisturised which made robbing him a little bit less of a chore.

'I'm so glad you liked your gift,' he nuzzled her neck.

'*Like* is an understatement.'

Zoë lovingly fondled the white gold, labradorite and diamond chandelier earrings. At *Le Mouton,* covetous female diners had polished their knives, ready to stab her and steal the jewels. She wasn't intimidated; she basked in the blatant jealousy.

'Hurry up,' she pleaded, as Josh fiddled to deactivate multiple alarm systems designed to keep the palace impenetrable to people pissed-off by the disparity in society. 'It's f-f-freezing out here.'

He opened the door. A wave of warmth hit them. Zoë got her second shock of the evening.

'Surprise!'

The scene was set for a surprise party. Interspersed by clusters of *Congratulations!* balloons, thirty guests grinned at her. Zoë was obviously the guest of honour. Glittery gold hearts dangled from the marble-and-glass staircase that spiralled up to an atrium. The stone floor was sprinkled with rose petals. Collages charting their relationship hid the starburst of colours in the three original Damien Hirst prints on the purple damask wallpaper. Beneath a dramatic crystal chandelier, the hall table showcased a four-tier celebration cake adorned with hand-piped chocolate roses.

'Babe,' Josh seized her hand. 'I've had the best six weeks of my life with you. It's been a thrill-a-minute. I've never met a girl who makes every day an adventure.'

Overawed, she gravitated towards the pyramid of champagne flutes and guzzled two helpings.

'You're flirty and fun,' he pursued Zoë. 'But, most importantly, you're not fickle. Knowing you *want* me rather than *need* me unlike the other parasites I've dated is an amazing feeling.'

Zoë choked on the creamy mousse of bubbles. Endlessly massaging his ego, hiking up her mini-skirts and wowing him with her acrobatics in the bedroom were key features of their relationship. But its foundation was the lie she had told. She'd learnt rich men were fed up with girls who got more turned on by their wallets than their wit. Leeches like her who sucked them dry. So she pretended that she was rich in her own right.

'I'm just disappointed that your family couldn't share this special occasion,' he went on.

To disguise the fact they weren't really multimillionaires, Zoë decided they spent most of the year overseas. Josh believed they were currently soaking up winter sun in Barbados. The factory workers from Birkenhead were a hundred times more likely to be swigging sangria on a package holiday to Benidorm.

'There's nothing sexier than a self-sufficient woman,' he concluded.

Avoiding eye contact, Zoë agreed with an exaggerated nod. It was wildly untrue. Splashing out cash provided the same adrenalin rush as when she diced with death down a country lane and her chronic spending had accumulated serious debts. Chased by credit card companies, bailiffs and HRMC, she'd stolen multiple identities – anyone who'd ever wronged her from a schoolteacher who failed her GCSE Maths exam to a catty rival at fashion college to a teenage boyfriend discovered shagging another girl behind the bike-sheds – and used their details to open bank accounts, obtain credit cards, qualify for loans and order a cornucopia of riches. But it was a high-risk strategy and the government was clamping down on fraudsters so Zoë know seducing a multi-millionaire was a more viable way of weathering this financial storm.

On his cue, Josh's sisters hung a huge banner over the marble banisters. Then her boyfriend knelt down, brandished a ring whose worth could easily have fed and watered a family for five years and repeated the question printed in italics.

'Zoë,' he asked, 'will you marry me?'

CHAPTER 1

Cupid had fired all his matchmaking arrows. The once-a-year mission to reignite romance was successfully complete. But the winged cherub had failed to convince all earthly citizens that love ranked superior to Louboutins.

"THE BEST THINGS IN LIFE ARE NOT FREE"

Zoë Hornby was a prime example as she unveiled the new design feature of her boutique.

'Shallow,' she admitted, 'but true.'

The wall stencil didn't just fill a blank space above the pay desk. Or provide a talking point for customers. Its main purpose was to debunk the myth that money couldn't buy happiness.

'The quote sends out the wrong message,' Charlotte argued, ritualistically dunking a chocolate biscuit into her mid-morning cup of tea, 'and it shouldn't occupy such a prominent position.'

'Don't frown,' the fashionista teased. 'It causes premature aging. Seriously unwise for a bride-to-be. Nobody wants wrinkles at a wedding.'

On the outskirts of Warrington, *Zoë's Zone* showed that suburban was not a synonym for subdued.

Today, the seasonal window display belonged to a naked, podgy and mischievous Cupid figurine surrounded by a harem of blow-up angels in faux fur minidresses. A mannequin styled as Venus, the Goddess of Love, complete with white toga and myrtle crown, frolicked on fluffy white scatter cushions like candyfloss clouds alongside taxidermied poodles that Zoë had dyed fluorescent pink. Under a decadent chandelier, the inside was also a profusion of pink and styled like a drag queen's boudoir. Glittery striped wallpaper, mirrored furniture and ropes of pearls and jewels. Silkscreen prints of Zoë in flirtatious poses hung in the individually-decorated changing cubicles (each named after a city that hosted its own fashion week) with 360^0 degree mirrors.

Outlandish garments – feather boas, flapper dresses and fedoras accessorised by imitation Fabergé eggs – were showcased on satin rails. The pricy merchandise was begged, stolen and borrowed from designers in Liverpool amidst Zoë's empty promises they would get a cut of the profits. Their patience was drying up like a river in a drought. Increasingly desperate, she had resorted to making low-budget replicas on her sewing machine including the lacy bustier that she now modelled with a leather miniskirt and stilettos.

'Material possessions don't keep you warm at night,' Charlotte insisted, fighting hard to defend love against two cynics who were in relationships out of convenience not choice.

'Cuddling,' Zoë said, facetiously, 'won't save you from hypothermia.'

'But central heating will,' Titty reinforced.

'So will an electric blanket.'

'Yes, all man-made inventions.'

'Jack and Rose were love's young dream,' Zoë referenced *Titanic*, 'but it didn't stop him perishing in the Atlantic.'

Despairing, Charlotte dug into the tin of Parisian macaroons that her friend had brought back from the City of Light. She always overindulged during times of turmoil. Another negative pregnancy test put comfort food on the menu. Her weight had ballooned recently. Unfortunately, the bulging belly gave John false optimism it might contain a baby not baked goods.

'Anyway,' Zoë picked a pistachio flavour, 'my engagement ring proves the quote isn't nonsense. I've never felt so ecstatic. Not even when I dabbled with legal highs for psychedelic inspiration as a fashion student.'

For the millionth time, she flaunted the whopping pink stone on a white gold band bracketed by shoulders of diamonds.

'It looks so heavy,' Charlotte said,

'A necessary evil,' Zoë explained, transfixed by the diamond as if it had hypnotic powers.

'You must need a hoist to lift your arm,' Charlotte giggled, referring to Titty's emerald-cut solitaire.

The doctor flinched. It was exquisite. A family heirloom, in fact, courtesy of Roderick's late grandmother. Lady Rutherford's marriage had lasted a lifetime. Titty hoped the ring was a good omen.

'It's crazy,' Zoë said, 'how we all got engaged on the same Valentine's Day.'

'Maybe John, Roderick and Josh were in cahoots?' Charlotte wondered.

'Roderick has no time for silly games,' Titty disparaged. 'He's been working in war-torn Africa since Christmas. Synchronising a proposal isn't really a priority when you're defending victims of genocide.'

'Well, then, maybe Cupid was in charge of our destinies,' she pointed at the chubby figurine.

'Cupid is a mythological creature.'

'Yes,' Zoë agreed, 'he's a figment of the imagination of women who can't accept love is a lie they tell themselves to feel less empty and alone. He's a gimmick created to sell soppy movies and Valentine's Day gift cards and Westlife ballads.'

'Cupid has two sets of arrows,' Charlotte educated her friend. 'Golden points to guarantee true, lasting love and lead-headed arrows for erotic love that is fun, but will fizzle out. Your heart was obviously shot with a lead tip.'

'Fine by me.'

In *Zoë's Zone*, subtlety was barred like a paedophile from a children's party. The current rotation of mannequins interspersing the changing cubicles wore embellished babydoll dresses, pink denim jackets and over-the-knee suede boots. Behind a holographic butterfly divider screen was the store cupboard. Since Zoë ran out of rent for her inner-city flat, she'd lived in this box room, her sleeping bag overcrowded by log-books and lace. But it hadn't curbed her spending habit.

This was curious, she admitted. A long time ago, she'd placated Titty by attending a Shopaholics Anonymous meeting and learnt one type of super spender didn't fit all. There were compulsive shopaholics like compulsive eaters who shopped to alleviate emotional distress; shopaholics who couldn't stop trawling the internet or traipsing around precincts until they'd found their version of perfection; shopaholics wanting an ego boost from flashing their cash; bargain seekers who purchased items simply because they were on sale; shoppers in an unhealthy cycle of buying and returning, similar to bulimics who gorged and purged; and collectors who had to stockpile items in every colour, size and combination.

If it was possible, Zoë embodied a new category of shopaholic. Like her bungee jumping adventure in New Zealand, rock climbing in Canada or road racing in Josh's convertible, she got an adrenaline rush from overspending. Her fingertips tingled, breathing rate ramped up and palms grew clammy when the final warnings from credit card companies or utility bills or overdraft statements came in the post. She got a thrill from reading the red letters, dodging the bailiffs, outsmarting HMRC with her hoaxes and scams. Adrenaline flooded her body and heightened her senses – hearing, vision, taste, smell, touch – and the euphoria lasted for hours.

'Josh designed this ring himself,' Zoë boasted to her friends on the purple chenille chaise longue.

'What a surprise,' Titty mocked, disapproving of the garish jewel.

'I realise Josh doesn't conform to the Oxbridge graduates in your social circle,' Zoë rolled her eyes smothered in pink shadow. 'Lawyers, bankers, doctors. Titled aristocrats. But he's a good guy which is a very rare breed these days.'

'He's a footballer,' Titty retorted. 'The two descriptions are mutually exclusive.'

'You've only met him twice.'

'That was two times too many.'

'Don't be a snob.'

'I just think you should aim higher.'

'No need. He meets the core criteria i.e. his pockets are deeper than the Grand Canyon and he's hot.'

'Only if you like metrosexual men.'

'What's wrong with a man who moisturises?'

'It's effeminate.'

'Remind us,' Charlotte interrupted, undercutting the tension, 'what's the cover story for this relationship?'

'I'm the daughter of self-made millionaires, Mike and Deirdre Fraser. Retired owners of *Sun on a Shoestring*, a budget travel company which brought Spanish seaside resorts to the masses. Their life is a permanent holiday since selling the business and they disowned me, their only child, because I wouldn't abandon my boutique and follow them to sunnier climes. The family feud means Mike and Deirdre won't be expected to contribute to the wedding costs so they'll fall entirely on Josh's shoulders.'

'How convenient.'

'Precisely.'

As always, Titty was stunned by her friend's audacious white lies. Zoë played men to the beat of her own drum, used and abused them. In contrast, she'd been with the same man for a decade, faultlessly faithful to Roderick, aware of the damning consequences for the Wedgewood-Beaverbrook reputation if she ever strayed. And Zoë put famous fraudsters to shame, the way she slipped between different identities and disguises to evade the consequences of her reckless spending.

Whereas Zoë got turned on by deceiving the taxman, Titty lived in fear of making a mistake and Charlotte's only brush with the law consisted of driving too slowly on the M6 motorway.

It was still hard to believe how the paths of three such different women had ever crossed. They'd met six years ago, knee-deep in mud in the queue for the toilets at another washed-out Glastonbury. Charlotte attended on a school trip; Titty was obliged to provide first-aid at the medical hut; Zoë, surprise surprise, had swindled tickets in the hope of catching the eye of a mega-rich musician with a bulging bank account. Yet, for all their quirks and qualms, opposites attracted and they brought out the best in each other.

'Sounds an excellent plan,' a customer emerged from the Milan changing cubicle's voile curtain.

Though it was teetering on the brink of insolvency, the boutique attracted a steady stream of loyal customers and Zoë had befriended this curvaceous pensioner. Thrice-married Margot was a glamour puss who ate men for dinner and scarpered with their credit cards before breakfast. Without children to call her own, Zoë had become a surrogate daughter, often a co-conspirator if Margot needed help to lure another man into her trap.

'Could I be mistaken for a Kardashian?' Margot twisted to examine her posterior.

'Yes, babe,' she reassured.

'Good, at least I won't have to spend the latest divorce settlement on buttock implants.'

Refusing to grow old gracefully, Margot's snow white hair was bouffant, a slick of red lipstick matched her false nails and weekly appointments with a sunbed meant she was tanned from top to tail as if sprayed in *Ronseal* wood stain.

'I'm having dinner with Dmitri,' she confided.

'The Russian oil baron that you snared on a Baltic cruise?'

'Yes, I need a dress that he'll never forget.'

'Then don't blend into the background,' Zoë said, as if it was possible in a lace appliqué body-con dress. 'Go for the hot pink version. Not black.'

Without further delay, Cheshire's sexiest septuagenarian as voted in a *Saga* poll followed her advice.

'Tempted to try it on, Charlotte?' the owner called, neatly folding the item into a branded bag.

'I reckon Brooklands Primary would lose its Ofsted "Outstanding" rating if I turned up to school dressed like a hooker.'

Zoë laughed, acutely aware that it would be ridiculous on the mumsy teacher who was dressed for comfort in a chunky knitted jumper dress, woolly tights and Mary Janes.

'Titty, you're not a fan, either?' she joked.

'I work in a hospital, Zoë, not on a catwalk.'

'Imagine wearing it on the wards,' Charlotte hooted, showering the plush sheepskin rug with crumbs.

'Yes, the last thing cardiac patients recovering from heart surgery need is a major shock to the system.'

The doctor preferred slacks to stilettos. Prim and proper, she wore tailored pieces for work and twin-sets and pearls for leisure. Her casual wardrobe consisted entirely of Lacoste, Brooks Brothers and Polo Ralph Lauren with plenty of tasselled loafers, Keds and boat shoes, pastels, polo shirts, cable knit cardigans and sweaters.

'Best be off,' Margot said.

'Oh, okay.'

'I'm so pleased for you, Zoë.'

'Thanks.'

'If you want any help to plan the wedding, let me know.'

'Will do.'

'Don't forget I can get you mates' rates with my divorce lawyer if Josh stops floating your boat. Amanda Cassidy, she's a legal shark. The most dastardly litigator in the city. Amanda can rip even the most lenient pre-nup to shreds to get you the biggest possible pay-off. She's bloodthirsty. Loves raw combat, fisticuffs, gloves off, teeth bared, claws sharp. Amanda's had a pathological hatred of men since her dad bedded her best friend and will eat, sleep and breathe a divorce lawsuit until the wife is victorious.'

'She sounds an appealing character,' Charlotte was sarcastic.

'Amanda's been the most useful weapon in my armoury for all three of my divorces,' Margot stated the facts.

'Okay,' Zoë nodded, 'I'll keep her in mind.'

Zoë's Zone was opposite a nursery. Mothers trussed up in Michelin-man padded coats pushed buggies and prams through its gates. Charlotte felt a surge of broodiness as she spied a little boy tugging his mum's scarf. He wouldn't let go. Oblivious to the stroppy screams, she watched the boy treat the scarf like an umbilical cord, wanting to preserve the connection with his mother that was threatened by nursery. The mother, however, was probably daydreaming about her life before these child-shaped problems as she heaved a sigh and crouched down to console him.

Perhaps it was easy for women like her to consider parenthood a rite of passage, a surety, something to take for granted. Charlotte knew it was a privilege because only a chosen few had the luxury. She doted on Chloe, but they weren't blood relations and she longed to experience that primeval love.

'Is John still firing blanks?' Zoë inquired, with the delicacy of a foghorn.

'That's not nice.'

'Problems with conceiving are inevitable when you date a man old enough to be your dad.'

'Not funny.'

'One in seven couples in this country have difficulty conceiving,' Titty bombarded them with medical statistics, 'which equates to approximately 3.5 million people.'

'Sorry, but I can't find much strength in numbers.'

'At 32,' Zoë took a kinder tone, 'you've still got plenty of time left on your biological clock so try not to stress.'

Titty checked her hospital pager.

'Isn't it your day off?' Charlotte asked.

'Technically.'

'You work way too hard.'

'Not if I'm competing for a consultancy post.'

'A consultancy post?'

'Yeah,' Zoë said, 'I always thought consultants had to be old and grey. Professorial types like your dad. Isn't it a bit early in your career?'

'A promotion will be tough, but not impossible,' she parroted Roderick.

Titty often did that. It had been a decade since the sounds she made belonged entirely to her. Perhaps even longer. It wasn't just Roderick in control of her voicebox; it was her parents, too. Like a non-stop express train, she'd always been bound for medicine. Detours to any other stations were strictly not allowed.

Her parents were eminent cardiothoracic surgeons. With her older brother incapacitated, Titty was heir apparent to the throne. Freewill didn't exist for the Wedgewood-Beaverbrook children. Her childhood home had been a shrine to surgery, teeming with books and artefacts and diagrams that her father drew by hand.

The drawing room at their ancestral seat, Thorn House, a Grade I listed stately home in rural Cheshire, doubled as a replica operating theatre equipped for a full dress rehearsal of all sorts of procedures. When other kids were learning about rainbows and dragons, Titty was practising the running stitch on a banana. Her 11th birthday present had been to transplant a sheep's heart bought from the local butcher into a sickly ewe. She'd asked for a Barbie doll.

'Roderick's a freak of nature,' Charlotte spoke the truth. 'Not everyone can be perfect all of the time. Give yourself a break.'

She smiled, gratefully, but the conversation was quickly hogged by a familiar topic.

'18K white gold…' Zoë rambled, reciting the ring's specifics that she had memorised over the past week.

Charlotte was unfazed that it dwarfed her heart-shaped equivalent. A boulder compared to a pebble. Her unease was caused by the risky arrangement.

'You know footballers have a terrible reputation for cheating,' she interrupted.

'I don't care if he plays the field. Excuse the pun. He's a means to an end. A get-out-of jail card.'

'Literally,' Titty feared her finances.

'We don't want you to get hurt,' Charlotte said.

'It's his wallet that I want.'

'But any kind of relationship based on deceit is doomed to fail.'

Hypocrisy halting the rant, Charlotte self-comforted with three slices of surplus chocolate cake leftover from her friend's engagement party.

'If you need cash,' Titty produced a pen, 'I can easily write you a cheque.'

'Thank you,' Zoë smiled, sincerely. 'But I'm a spendaholic. Not a charity case.'

CHAPTER 2

'Pretty, pretty please,' Charlotte begged the plastic stick to reveal that miracles did happen.

Thirty seconds was the recommended waiting time. She'd been staring at the stick for two-hundred-and-thirty seconds with laser beams of intent as if concentrated effort could conjure up a positive result. Still just one blue line. Still not pregnant. Yet again, her only paltry consolation was the product had a 0.01% chance of being wrong.

After collecting Chloe from her first meeting, she had taken the test in the Girl Guides' outdoor toilet hut that was exposed to the elements. No roof meant a nippy breeze chapped her bare buttocks as she'd done the all-important wee and a slug peeped out of the cistern and her red patent wellies were dirtied by mud and muck from the biodegradable floor.

'Hurry up,' her stepdaughter said, knocking the flimsy wooden door.

'Just a second,' Charlotte wiped her tears with screwed-up toilet roll.

'Come on!'

'Almost ready.'

Charlotte tossed the latest failure in the compost bin. If only getting rid of the disappointment that originated in her heart and spread its tentacles into every bone, sinew, artery, of her body could be achieved so easily. Tossing it away was more like tossing a Highland caber.

Wedged in the stall designed for kids with hips half the width of hers, Charlotte struggled to pull up her knickers with a granny-style gusset before her stepdaughter called again and she scampered out to the car park set within 350 hectares of a Cheshire conservation area.

Home to a diversity of habitats, the parkland on the periphery of the Peak District was popular with activity enthusiasts. Its man-made lake was currently the training ground for amateur canoeists who dared to practise a capsizing manoeuvre as coots and cormorants swooped down to the water's edge scouting for pike, perch, roach and eels. A windsurfer caused a splash when a jump went spectacularly wrong much to the chagrin of a cluster of sailing boats whose crew got drenched like the participants in the ALS ice bucket challenge. Nearer the car park, kids had fun on a zip wire connecting two treehouses in the boughs of mature oak trees while others experimented with falconry or archery.

'Got the stop watch?' Chloe asked.

'Yep.'

'And the whistle?'

'Yep.'

Chloe had to skip for exactly two minutes – switching feet, front to back, criss-crossed hands – to qualify for the level one sports commendation. Her rope whipped the mulchy leaves underfoot into a frenzy. The gusty wind slapped them against her face. But the little girl overcame the odds to win her first honour.

'I did it,' she shrieked, cartwheeling over the uneven ground in celebration.

With hands numbed by the cold, Charlotte applauded the child whose chipmunk cheeks were rosy from the exercise.

'You're a star,' she smiled, pinning the fabric badge to her Girl Guides blazer.

'Guides is awesome,' Chloe said, asking Charlotte to plait her long, dark hair while they waited for John's ex-wife.

'Oh, good, I'm so pleased that you enjoyed it.'

'You come up with the best ideas.'

Over the years, Chloe had excelled at her elite private school – from lacrosse captain to prize short-story teller to musical maestro – yet the simple skipping achievement thrilled her like no other. Probably because it was independent, without hours of tuition or interference from her high-maintenance mother.

'When can we go shopping for bridesmaid dresses?' Chloe babbled.

'Um... soon.'

'I'm so excited.'

'Mmm, me, too.'

'Can we go to the big shops in Liverpool?'

'Yes, alright.'

For Charlotte, no baby meant no wedding. They were inextricably linked. Marriage was the framework for a family. If she couldn't fell pregnant, the chapel bells would never chime.

'Actually,' Chloe declared. 'I've already found my dress.'

'Oh, really?'

'Yes, it's Cinderella-style. Dusky blue with sparkly ballet pumps. It's perfect, too, because you're as beautiful as a Disney princess and daddy's your Prince Charming.'

'Mmm, sounds great.'

Unsettled, Charlotte headed for *Café Culture*, hopeful cake would be a cure for her upset. The park patrol was adept at managing the snow dumped over the Peak District during winter and had gouged a functional path through sludge towards the tea room. It was bustling with hikers on the Cheshire Three Peaks Challenge who were ravenous after burning off copious calories. They'd devoured the chocolate fudge cake, Victoria sponge and lemon tart so she bought herself a Belgian bun instead and narrowly avoided a segway as she rejoined Chloe at a picnic bench by the lake.

'Can I have a bite?'

'No, Chloe, your mother would go mad.'

'Then I won't tell her.'

'That's a euphemism for lying.'

'Pleeeease…'

Putty in those puppy-dog eyes, Charlotte swiftly broke off a squidgy corner of the bun. Her stepdaughter was raised on a vegan diet with strict sugar rations. It was all an attempt at pomp and circumstance by her mother, Horatia, a blatant social climber.

'Daddy says you're trying for a baby,' Chloe threw in a casual remark.

Charlotte was blindsided. Her fiancé had vowed to stay schtum when parenthood was merely a dream. She wasn't even sure if Chloe had endured the birds and bees talk. His mistake guaranteed more casualties of her lie.

'Am I going to be a big sister?' she chirped, tingling with excitement.

'Erm,' Charlotte blew her runny nose, 'it's in the planning stages. Very early days. Not everyone is lucky enough to be a mum so you mustn't get your hopes up.'

'But a baby would be super cool.'

'Really?'

'Yep.'

'Even though it can be a big upheaval?' she pounced on any hidden doubts.

Chloe's caterpillar brows not yet tamed by tweezers knitted with confusion.

'They change the dynamic of a family. Sharing your dad might be a difficult adjustment. And babies scream, cry, soil their nappies. Not forgetting the vomit.'

'Yuk,' Chloe grimaced, wrinkling her snub nose as her stepmum described the stench in deliberately grotesque detail.

'I always wanted to be an only child,' Charlotte pretended, though she had adored the happy chaos of being sandwiched in a family of four kids.

'Yeah, it's not too bad, but I get really lonely sometimes. I have lots of friends, but it's not the same. Mummy only lets me have a playdate between 3p.m. and 4p.m. on Saturdays. I wouldn't have to book time to see a brother or sister.'

'But being an only child,' she made Chloe laugh, 'means John and I get to spoil you rotten.'

Charlotte felt her reef knot of anxiety unwind. Grossly distorting the experience had successfully deterred her stepdaughter. But she had a horrible hunch that notions of a new sibling would rear their ugly gargoyled heads once again.

'Hello,' Horatia sniffed with haughty indignation as her Range Rover slammed to a stop only inches from their feet.

The black metallic beast with two turbo exhausts, four litre diesel engine and three-zone climate control intimidated other motorists. So did its driver. Charlotte's polar opposite was a high-flying stockbroker. Everything apart from making money bored her. Men were moronic; children were a chore; housework was hell. In Horatia's kingdom, academia reigned supreme, but only because it enhanced her social status.

When Chloe's pressure cooker boiled over, Charlotte was its emergency release. A foil to Horatia's incessantly high standards, she taught Chloe that life meant more than exam papers. They had bonded over sewing patchwork quilts for refugees, trips to the seaside where they explored amoebic life forms in rock pools and tending to her cottage garden.

Deigning to lower the tinted window, Horatia's square bob was inky black and cut to accentuate her razor-sharp cheekbones. Her hawk nose protruded from under a blunt fringe. Whereas Charlotte was a plump mother hen, children flocking to her like chicks, Horatia was a bird of prey, always on the hunt for her next victim. Nothing escaped her beady-eyed attention. Chloe hurriedly licked her lips free of sugar granules.

'Sorry I'm late,' she said, curling her mean mouth into a smile that stank of insincerity. 'I had to finalise a multi-million dollar deal before I left the office.'

'No problem.'

'I suppose the closest you come to stress is trying to decipher a 6-year-old's scrawling handwriting.'

'Mmm,' she complied, secretly speculating her stress-o-meter was dangerously high after the failed pregnancy test.

Dressed to kill, Horatia wore a black suit jacket constructed with peaked shoulders and lapels and cigarette pants. Her perfume was overpowering. Sultry base notes reduced her male colleagues to mush. A vixen, it was a ploy to manipulate the weaklings.

The only man she'd ever loved was John. He used to be a banker for a rival firm. They were the ultimate power couple, splashing big bonuses on bolthole apartments in every capital city and Bollinger and vacations in the Bahamas, until he grew tired of the cutthroat corporate world and of his wife. Horatia had sneakily flushed her birth control pills down the toilet to trap him into staying married, but he saw Chloe was a con and they split before her 3-month pregnancy scan. John returned to history, his first love, and met his soulmate, Charlotte, at a national teachers' conference.

'Horatia, it's lovely to see you,' Charlotte was unerringly polite.

'I wish I could say it was mutual.'

'Mummy, I got a badge,' Chloe trilled.

'Oh?'

'For skipping.'

'I'm sure Oxbridge is desperate for students who can skip.'

'Actually, I've heard skipping can clinch an application,' Charlotte was jovial.

'The dumbing down of our education system is a terrible thing,' Horatia scorned, tutting as Chloe ran off to chase a squirrel.

Charlotte had no axe to grind with the pompous ex-wife. She saw only the good qualities in people, blessed with an internal filter that blocked out the bad even if Horatia thought schoolteachers were second-class citizens. Her most recent gripe centred on girl guiding which she labelled a pathetic substitute for after-school chess.

'I don't understand how a teacher can be anti-education,' she prattled.

'I'm not anti-education,' Charlotte clarified for the umpteenth time. 'I'm pro-choice. If Chloe wants to study law or politics or finance, she has my full support, but I don't think children should be forced to follow a path that makes them miserable. Education is about opportunity. Broadening Chloe's horizons. Not limiting them to a certain few careers that you deem acceptable.'

'Be honest,' she dismissed, 'you're a primary school teacher because it was the only job you're capable of doing.'

'No, I wanted to nurture the next generation.'

'Rubbish. You couldn't make a living out of housewifery or cooking or cleaning – God knows the market's saturated with domestic goddesses – so the last remaining option was to teach times tables to little kids.'

Charlotte refused to play this spiteful game. *Sticks and stones may break my bones but words will never hurt me*, she recited the phrase under her breath, but Horatia proceeded to use words as weapons and they were more lethal than a lance.

'Still barren?' she inquired. 'Infertility is a terrible cross to bear. Try not to feel utterly useless. As though you've failed as a woman. Of course, one night without contraception was all it took to conceive Chloe.'

Horatia inserted a pause that forced her nemesis to reflect on her inadequacies.

'Well,' the ex-wife sighed, 'perhaps it's a sign.'

'A sign of what?'

'You're not meant to be a mother.'

Content with the caustic remark, she beckoned Chloe and spattered the lowly teacher with more mud as they sped off to a violin recital.

CHAPTER 3

With a flurry of activity, Titty rushed to lend her services to the staff wheeling a stretcher onto the cardiac ward.

'I...can't...breathe,' the emergency patient clutched her chest which felt encased in a block of concrete.

Drip fed the key details from paramedics, Titty listened to her airway and made a speedy diagnosis. It was a heart attack. Harriet Taylor required urgent surgery.

'Stay calm,' she instructed, turning up the flow of oxygen to her mask.

But it was highly unrealistic halfway through a heart attack when each breath was a battle.

'Ms Taylor,' she addressed the sufferer with characteristic bluntness, 'we have to perform surgery to open the blocked artery and restore blood flow or you'll die.'

Writhing in agony, the patient's consent was instant.

•

'Good morning,' Titty pulled back the pencil pleat curtain of her cubicle.

Dr Wedgewood-Beaverbrook crawled into the groggy patient's focus. Titty was in classic work mode – a diamond pendant in the open collar of her pristine white shirt, navy pencil skirt and black heels. Harriet's gaze widened to the ward. She saw flickering halogen lights, nurses comforting weary relatives, portable IV drips squeaking over linoleum floors.

'Am I alive?' she croaked.

'Yes.'

'What a relief, I'm too busy to die.'

Before donning a generic off-white hospital gown, 58-year-old Harriet Taylor's sartorial style had been a throwback to the 80s, the decade when she first broke the corporate glass ceiling. Permed hair, lashings of blue mascara, huge round spectacles and gold hooped earrings were teamed with a cobalt blue power suit whose padded shoulders made her the shape of an inverted triangle and added a look of brusque efficiency.

But there was nothing old-fashioned about her attitude. Harriet Taylor hadn't just broken the glass ceiling; she'd used a mallet to smash it into a thousand tiny, insignificant shards. The head of a billion-dollar multinational technology company, Ms Taylor was a trailblazer for gender equality, empowering women worldwide with her refusal to be defined by her XX chromosomes.

Titty recognised Harriet Taylor from *Forbes*' annual list of most powerful women. The CEO was notorious for commuting between the UK and the US every week, snatching just a few hours of jet-lagged sleep before speaking to thousands of employees either at the headquarters in Washington D.C or Liverpool about her pioneering plans to quadruple profits.

'Where's my mobile?' she interrogated, a slave to her job even in the aftermath of her heart attack.

'Um…'

'I must check my e-mails.'

'Ms Taylor, I need your undivided attention.'

'Not now.'

'It's very important.'

'It can wait.'

'You don't have the luxury of time.'

The statement finally applied the brakes to her feverish hunt rifling through the bags on the bedside cabinet.

'Your attack was severe,' Titty delivered the news. 'The coronary angioplasty was a case of damage control. Your heart muscle sustained extensive injuries.'

Colour drained from her cheeks until she resembled the cadavers in the morgue a few floors below.

'However, it doesn't have to be a death sentence. I will prescribe clot-busting medication. Changes to your diet and lifestyle can also make a massive difference.'

'I won't retire,' Ms Taylor waved her hands in protest as she pre-empted the first piece of advice.

'Work-related stress is known to contribute to heart problems. If retirement is too hasty, you should consider delegating.'

Wincing, the idea caused physical pain.

'Perhaps you'll consider our cardiac rehabilitation centre?'

'Not a chance,' she dismissed the information leaflet as if it were an irritating fly.

'At least take some time off to recover.'

'*Time off?*'

Yes, it may take several months before you can manage a full day of work.'

'Being busy is the best medicine,' she said, stubbornly rejecting the doctor's orders. 'A holiday would kill me.'

Titty floundered. Despite sacrificing her twenties for medical school, gruelling placements and specialist training, quitting had never been an option. Nor had taking time off. She couldn't berate the patient for prioritising her career.

'Is there anyone I can call for you?' she asked, flicking to the next-of-kin section of the notes.

'No.'

'A spouse, child, friend?'

'No.'

'A work colleague?'

'I said no, doctor, don't ask again.'

•

Only the strongest, blackest espresso would cure Titty's chronic fatigue. It wasn't caused simply by a string of 16-hour shifts. She had been manically revising for consultancy exams.

'Just what I fancy,' Dr Richard Lam swiped the cup from her grasp.

An almighty yawn shuddering her senses, Titty glowered at the bespectacled registrar who updated cardiac charts at the nurses' station. He was the bane of her existence. A do-gooder whose popularity dwarfed hers.

No-one at work liked her. Neither peers nor patients. Professor Wedgewood-Beaverbrook, Titty's father, was the hospital's clinical lead so allegations of nepotism were rife. They were all true. Her surname had given her a massively unfair advantage.

As the lynchpin of the class system, her aloofness didn't help. She turned down every after-work drinks invite, Christmas party, attempt at chitchat in the on-call room. As Roderick had stated, *friends were a waste of space unless they helped you skip rungs on the career ladder.*

'Three all-nighters in one week,' Richard said, as Titty operated the noisy machine for a replacement espresso.

Richard Lam childishly shook the machine while she placed a paper cup under the nozzle.

'Yes,' she boasted, 'I deserve a gold star.'

'Or your head examined. Making life-and-death decisions while pumped full of caffeine is not sensible. And adrenalin isn't a substitute for decent rest.'

Under pressure to push boundaries, Titty dismissed the criticism.

'It's a shame leave isn't transferrable,' he said. 'You must have amassed a record amount.'

'Six months, to be precise, but I wouldn't lend a single second to you.'

'*You'll* need the pity party when I beat you in the race for consultant,' Dr Lam was unscathed.

'In your dreams.'

'No matter how many hours you work, Dr Wedgewood-Beaverbrook, or how much daddy pays his contacts on the board of governors, you'll always lack the most important qualification for a cardiothoracic surgeon.'

'Which is what?'

'To have a heart made of muscle, not tin.'

'Well, your confidence is completely misguided. Half the hospital knows about your gambling habit.'

'Waging an annual bet on the Grand National is a hobby, not a habit,' he insisted. 'Unlike you, I have a life outside this ward. The appraisal panel will agree it's a much healthier approach.'

'Admitting you have a problem is the first step,' she patronised.

While the caffeine recharged her batteries, Titty spurned fantasies about a sabbatical. She could read a novel for the first time since school. Visit Asia. Join a netball team. Then she checked her iPhone.

No new messages

Women would bend over backwards until their spine snapped for a fiancé like Roderick. One who didn't throw a tantrum if they were late home or forgot the groceries. Just occasionally, though, it would be nice if he registered her absence. Sent a signal that he missed her. Even if it was in Morse code.

'Damn,' Titty muttered, noticing the urgent page.

'Is daddy calling?'

'Bore off, Richard.'

'Run along, don't keep daddy waiting.'

'He's Professor Bartholomew Wedgewood-Beaverbrook to you.'

'Ugh, it's such a mouthful, no wonder he gets abbreviated to Bart the Beaver.'

It was true that Professor Wedgewood-Beaverbrook did not tolerate tardiness. Abandoning her coffee, she hurriedly navigated the busy corridors to her father's office, but it was like swimming upstream. Going against the flow of human traffic took time and she arrived slightly behind schedule. Knocking to enter, she felt like a schoolgirl gingerly approaching the headmaster's room, expecting a rollicking.

'You're late,' he complained.

'Only by two minutes.'

'*Late*, adverb. Definition: to do something after the expected, proper, or usual time. Be that two minutes or twenty minutes, Titty, the fact is you're late.'

'But it's visiting hours,' she panted. 'The hospital is swarming. I couldn't push people out of the way.'

Professor Wedgewood-Beaverbrook tutted. For an eminent cardiac surgeon, he, too, was not a man of much heart and Titty highly suspected he'd have bulldozed his way through the crowds to get somewhere on time. Neither generation chose this medical speciality for sentimental reasons. To them, the heart was a pump. Universal associations with emotion, thought, will, got dismissed. The lure was the challenge of its complex anatomy.

Regal in a double breasted pinstripe suit, Professor Wedgewood-Beaverbrook was exceptionally tall. It made sense given he looked down on much of society. At 60, he was debonair and a font of knowledge. Crows' feet imbued him with an air of infinite wisdom. He had a sprinkling of age spots over his aquiline nose and a jawline that could cut bone with more accuracy than a surgical saw. His white hair was flamboyantly swept over to one side, pronouncing the widow's peak, and juxtaposed by bushy dark eyebrows slanted into a frown of consternation.

The clinical lead's office intimidated visitors. On his solid oak desk, photos chronicled his dalliances with Prime Ministers outside 10 Downing Street where he'd lavished them with million-pound cheques to buy a disproportionately large vote in elections; Presidents Bush, Clinton and Obama on the White House lawn during a stint as the presidential surgeon; Christmasses with the Queen at Balmoral. Sliding bookcases flaunted award-winning medical journals he had written; the mantelpiece housed his Nobel Prize for innovative embryonic stem cell research; certificates of excellence and honorary degrees from Ivy League institutes filled every spare section of fleur-de-lys wallpaper.

A relic from her childhood, Professor Wedgewood-Beaverbrook's office also displayed an ornamental porcelain head of the 19th-century discipline of phrenology. It revolved around the idea that different areas of the mind had different mental faculties. A person's skull size could then be measured to determine the capacity for various attributes. One junior doctor criticised by Professor Wedgewood-Beaverbrook had made a defamatory mock-up from various foodstuffs. The nastiness portion was a melon; the generosity portion was a pea. He was fired with the same projectile ruthlessness of a ball out of a cannon.

'Please sit,' her father instructed, their exchange steeped in its usual formality.

'Thank you.'

Only then, as Titty settled on the stiff Chesterfield armchair, did she notice the room was sliced into shards of sunlight. It must have been daytime. Time was distorted by her irregular shift patterns. She did not rise and set with the sun or eat the three meals that defined the day and the artificially-lit hospital entrenched her confusion.

Liverpool General Hospital looked over the city metropolis. Street noise floated through the open window – fire engine sirens, people chatting outside grand civic buildings, babies wailing to be freed from their prams. In the distance, ferries escorted commuters between Liverpool and the Wirral. Football fans making the pilgrimage to Anfield spilled out of Lime Street station ready for a stadium tour. Workers targeted Sefton Park in their lunchbreak. The green space was an antidote to a congested, manic morning spent inside four walls staring at PowerPoint presentations and spreadsheets. It was the lungs of the city, a place to breathe. She hadn't wandered around a park for years.

'Dr Wedgewood-Beaverbrook, I have received your application for the consultancy post,' he began.

'Yes, papa,' Titty said, rubbing her eyes raw from the lack of sleep.

She prepared for a barrage of criticism that harked back to his days as an Army lieutenant. But it didn't show up. Her delight was tinged with suspicion.

'You are a strong candidate.'

'Gosh, thank you.'

'Quiet, Titania, I'm still speaking.'

'Sorry, papa.'

'Your mother and I have been impressed by your recent behaviour,' he continued. 'Accepting Roderick's proposal showed great maturity and the whole family will be overjoyed when you become *Liverpool General*'s youngest ever consultant.'

Growing up as a daughter of ambitious surgeons, praise was not a common currency and the exchange rate was pitifully low. Even winning a place at Oxford hadn't warranted a congratulations card yet she was supposed to sing their praises left, right and centre. His belief in her prodigious talent meant the tiny spark of desire to take a holiday had been extinguished.

'It's wonderful to hear that you believe I can triumph on my own merit,' Titty gushed.

'No, you misunderstand.'

'Oh?'

'I have a meeting wth the board of governors this afternoon. It will be an ideal opportunity to drop a few subtle hints why applicant Titania Wedgewood-Beaverbrook is right for the role. Failing this strategy, threatening to withdraw the family's funding for the new cardiology wing should change their minds.'

Titty felt glum. Her own father, a man biologically programmed to think she was the bee's knees, was telling her that she would fail without his input. Bribing the board wasn't fair on her or her colleagues.

It's not cheating, Roderick's words rang in her ears, *it's commitment to the cause*. Once again, she made the mistake of listening.

CHAPTER 4

Rockingham Palace was no longer a bachelor pad. Twelve hours ago, Josh followed the proposal with keys to his mansion. Zoë was gobsmacked by her good fortune and immediately made the move.

It couldn't have come a moment too soon. This morning, Zoë had read the *Cheshire Chronicle*. Self-obsessed, she didn't often bother with news of other people, but this particular front-page had anchored her attention.

```
IDENTITY THEFT IS NOT A VICTIMLESS CRIME
```

As part of the county council's crackdown, it was an investigative report about a recent spate of criminality. Joy Stratton, the slapper behind the bike-sheds with her teenage boyfriend, was the victim in question.

Zoë didn't feel a trace of guilt. She marvelled at her own ingeniousness. Aware Joy was a Beatles aficionado, she'd set up a fake website purporting to sell signed memorabilia of the famous four. Willingly providing her debit card details including the 3-digit security code on the back, she'd fallen hook, line and sinker for the con before realising £2,000 not £200 was missing from her account. And Ringo Starr's drumstick wasn't in the mail.

So what if Joy's nest egg was wiped out, life had been ruined, relationship degraded by misplaced accusations of theft… Perhaps, in a warped way, this was Zoë's way of policing the local community. Teaching traitors a lesson. An unscrupulous sort of divine justice. Or she was just greedy with a skewed set of morals.

In the Joy Stratton case, she'd committed fraud by setting up a fake website. It wasn't her only hijack technique. Often, in the dead of night, she riffled like a cat burglar through rubbish bins for unshredded bank statements, credit card statement, CVs or even fashion catalogues stamped with names, addresses and account numbers of people in her black books. These details were also useful for piecing together PINs and passwords. Sometimes, she phished for sensitive information by sending legitimate-looking emails from reputable companies requesting bank details.

Tailoring her scams to her victims, Zoë was riotously successful.

It was staggering how gullible Mr Hilliard, her cantankerous school maths tutor, had been the time she'd given him a chance to win a Harley Davidson.

```
    Bored with the bus? she'd typed. Cooped up in
your car? Tired of taking the train? Free your
   spirt with a motorbike. We're giving away a
     brand new Harley Davidson to one lucky
  supermarket customer. Simply click the link
    below, fill in your details and you'll be
     automatically entered for our prize draw.
```

The sales pitch was a masterstroke for two reasons. First, it had preyed on his frugality. Mr Hilliard wasn't nicknamed Scrooge for nothing. Second, it had preyed on his petrol-head passion that Zoë had inadvertently discovered when she'd found an Autotrader brochure hidden inside his trigonometry textbook.

For a mathematician, he wasn't quick at doing the maths. It took him six months to realise £6,000 had been extracted from his current account and, quoting probability, he had a greater chance of being run over by a *Harley Davidson* than riding one. She'd bolted long before the authorities got involved.

Damn, Zoë sighed, scanning the tips on how to thwart con artists like her. Top of the list was checking credit reports. Shredding sensitive documents before binning them. Leaving important documents at home in a safe place. Redirecting post for at least a year after moving home.

Thankfully, Zoë's criminal escapades were consigned to her past. That phase of her chequered life was done and dusted. Her future unfolded here, at *Rockingham Palace*, although she expected withdrawal symptoms from the adrenalin rush of danger. She'd have to find a different outlet for her addiction that didn't risk prison.

'Woah,' Zoë said, entering the house she could confidently call home.

Plagued by worries of outstaying her welcome, the fashionista had spent just a handful of nights here until now. And her explorations had been hindered by Josh's presence. Today's match in Rome solved that problem. The freedom wasn't squandered. But she made a mental note to restrain her reaction upon Josh's return because he believed she owned a swanky penthouse apartment in Liverpool's docklands so she ought to act used to living in the lap of luxury.

'*Big Brother*,' she clapped to activate his 60-inch plasma TV in the octagonal lounge that overlooked two acres of landscaped grounds.

Boxwood hedges sculpted into topiary screened the hot tub from prying paparazzi who frequently circled in helicopters for a salacious snap. A towering jet fountain spouting from the ornamental lake stocked with koi carp was the focal point. Purple Japanese maples stood sentinel in square pots of grey gravel to frame the decked patio. Sleek silver chairs surrounded a fire pit filled with iridescent glass pebbles. Layered by height, spiky shrubs bordered the lawn mown in graduating vertical stripes. Smaller cobalt blue and lime green grasses studded hexagonal flowerbeds.

Woah, Zoë repeated, charting the differences between this palace and the sprawl of flats where she'd grown up. Unlike Titty's abode that was brimming with butlers and maids, her dilapidated council estate had been ripe for refurbishment.

Serviced by a crappy pub that sold nothing but pints and pork scratchings, she'd loathed the poky flat with broken furniture singed by her mum's cigarette butts and a kitchen table pimpled with chewing gum. The only outdoor space had been a paved courtyard covered with pigeon droppings.

'Ooh, heaven really is a place on Earth,' she squealed with delight at the sunken marble tub in the downstairs bathroom that trounced her boutique's 4ftx2ft store cupboard.

'But you're no angel.'

'Excuse me?'

Busy on the all-access tour, Zoë had been impervious to the removal men struggling with her crates of clothes. Most were straight out of storage. Impersonating Joy Stratton had also paid for a year's contract at the local lock-up and go.

'Would it to kill you to help?' one moaned, rightly presuming money bred idleness.

'No, but it might break a nail.'

'You won't be so glib if I fall down the stairs.'

'Wrong,' she corrected, 'my fiancé can easily pay the compensation.'

Elevated by over-the-knee grey suede boots from her boutique, Zoë trotted into the bespoke kitchen and snapped pictures on her smartphone to circulate to friends.

Of the nine reception rooms, this open-plan mecca of modernity had the most *wow* factor. Aubergine gloss cabinets edged by a silver trim. Top-of-the-range integrated appliances, chrome handles, granite worktops. Pots and pans on exposed rails gleamed under recessed spotlights. Silver spray-painted apples and pears accessorised the fluted fruit bowl. Further in the distance, crushed velvet purple sofas artfully surrounded another TV that doubled as a home cinema. It was nailed to a feature wall of football trophies and shirts. An ultra-modern smoky glass dining table on stainless steel legs comfortably seated twenty adults beneath purple-and-silver pendant lights that could be controlled remotely from any room in the house.

Adjunct to the kitchen, behind floor-to-ceiling frosted glass panes, she investigated the indoor pool with folding roof and pared down her celebratory dance (a mix of the Harlem Shake and Gangnam style) upon noticing the security cameras in all communal spaces.

'Ah!' Zoë exclaimed, spotting a figure rapping the panel of bi-fold doors that retracted into the wall cavity.

Dripping in diamonds, it obviously wasn't the gardener. Josh had three sisters. But they weren't so flash. Nor did a woman dressed like an off-duty supermodel with stud earrings the size of ice-cubes and a dark red Balenciaga leather biker jacket with black sequined lapels, black leggings and leopard-print Louboutin boots seem an escapee from the local loony bin. Unless she was a kleptomaniac who had robbed Cheshire's top boutiques.

'Open the door,' the women mouthed.

'Um…'

'Hurry up, it's parky out here.'

For the first time, Zoë didn't resent the grumpy removal men. She hoped they weren't too pissed off to rescue her if the unexpected visitor wielded an axe. Though it was impossible to conceal any weapon down those drainpipe leggings.

'Sophie Stanford,' she extended a bejewelled hand that excited Zoë's magpie traits. 'My husband Pete is Josh's teammate. We live next-door.'

Now Zoë recognised the WAG – aged 28, the Liverpudlian had gained independent fame as a glamour model and released a fitness DVD on how she blitzed excess baby weight and reclaimed her bikini body just thirty days after giving birth to twins, Chardonnay and Champagne. Caked in make-up, her surgically-enhanced features were accented by permanent liner, inches of foundation, one rigid expression due to an overdose of fillers. Artificial beat *au naturel* into pulp.

'Loving your style,' Sophie complimented, stroking the chic printed blouse with bell sleeves that Zoë had purchased in lieu of a month's electricity.

'Thanks, it's YSL,' she replied.

'Yes, that's right, I posted it on Instagram when I first spotted it during New York fashion week.'

'Those jeans really enhance your thigh gap,' Zoë returned the praise.

'I've just bought a new ellipsis machine for our home gym and it's worked wonders on my glutes.'

'Take a seat,' she ushered Sophie to a black leather stool at the kitchen island.

Somewhere, a removal man dislocated his shoulder trying to haul a hundred shoe boxes into the dressing room, but neither WAG had a smidgen of desire to help.

'Fancy a brew?' Zoë asked, a pleasurable shiver when her engagement ring clinked the taps as she boiled the supersonic kettle.

'No, thanks, I'm on a detox. A pint of salt water each morning, cayenne pepper throughout the day and a laxative tea at night. It's an extreme low-calorie diet with ingredients known to speed up metabolism.'

'Sure I can't tempt you with a fondant fancy?' she brandished the plate of colour-coordinated white and dark sponges.

Sophie recoiled as if they were poison. It was obvious from her stick-insect proportions that calories were classed an enemy whereas Zoë treated food like it was going out of fashion. She didn't discriminate. Any culture, cuisine, if it was edible, she ate it, with the possible exception of caviar.

'You don't seriously eat those repulsive 300 calorie-a-pop cakes guaranteed to make you morbidly obese?' she flicked her tousled hair like a blonde waterfall that tumbled down her coat.

'Nope,' Zoë faked, ignoring the gruff voice of another manual labourer at the end of his tether.

'They're just a decorative accent?'

'That's right.'

Reaching for the sleek teacup, Zoë knocked a saucer onto the tiles with underfloor heating. Its fragile china shattered. She crouched down to tidy the mess which was tough wearing a restrictive leather miniskirt so tight that it nearly cut off her circulation.

'Babe,' Sophie interrupted, 'don't risk housewives' knee. Get the maid to clean up.'

'The maid?'

'Yeah, haven't you met Barbara?'

'Barbara?'

On Sophie's cue, a downtrodden woman arrived on the scene with a dustpan and brush. It transpired Josh hired a team of help. Including a French chef trained at *Le Cordon Bleu* whom Zoë was dying to exploit.

'Are you a fan of Cardio Craze exercise classes?' Sophie pulled out a diary from the folds of her cavernous handbag.

Zoë hoped her ignorance wasn't too transparent. She didn't do exercise. Manning the store alone from dawn until dusk (paying staff was totally implausible) meant she needed frequent sugar fixes. And she vastly preferred scoffing biscuits to burning them off. Plus, sweat and style didn't mix. Not that it deterred her from buying Stella McCartney's latest gym collection.

'Of course I'm a fan,' she said, laughing like it was a rhetorical question.

'There's a class every Thursday at the local gym, super workout, and the instructor has Rosie Huntington-Whiteley on speed dial.'

'Seriously?'

'Uh-huh.'

'She's my idol.'

'Me, too,' Sophie confessed.

'Then it's a date.'

Encouraging the maid to search for microscopic pieces of china, Zoë counted the days until Thursday, the day of Cardio Craze.

WAGs represented her two favourite things – power and privilege – and infiltrating their community was a lifelong aim. Like a pig in very expensive muck, she wallowed in the latest triumphant chapter of this rags to riches story.

CHAPTER 5

Outside the classroom, sunlight fractured the cloud cover to end the persistent cold snap. Its rays speckled the assortment of tulips that Charlotte and her pupils had planted in the playground. Beds of buttercup yellow bulbs pushed through the soil to mingle with pure whites, shell pinks, silky purple blooms and magentas.

'Walking to school,' Charlotte clapped the suggestion with endless enthusiasm.

'My mummy always makes me turn off the tap when I brush my teeth.'

'Well done, Poppy, reducing water wastage is another great way to save the planet.'

Seated in a semi-circle, the children were enjoying a geography lesson at Brooklands Primary School. It was a typical classroom – whiteboard, reams of paper, trays of felt tips, chewed pencils and colouring pens – with a few personal touches. One wall was commandeered by a Tudor project – last term, her class had performed a potted history of Henry the Eighth for proud parents – and bean bags made Charlotte's reading corner a comfy place to snuggle with a story.

'Recycling?'

'Yes, Sophia, recycling items we don't want anymore is a really good idea.'

'Does that mean I can recycle my cat?'

'Your cat?'

'Yeah,' she said, whirling her candyfloss blonde hair into a top knot, 'Coco scratched me and I don't want him anymore.'

Charlotte smiled, wryly. She loved teaching 6-year-olds. They were at a special stage of development, acquiring a more mature understanding of the world yet still at the age of speaking without editing, often providing refreshingly honesty perspectives or hysterically candid commentaries on their home life.

'I'm pretty sure cats shouldn't be recycled,' she replied.

'Oh.'

'Why might Coco have lashed out?'

'Because I sat on him.'

'Ah, well, Coco scratched you because he felt scared, not because he meant to hurt you.'

'Maybe.'

'If you take a bit more care where you sit, you'll probably become the best of friends.'

A bell truncated their lesson.

'Right, girls and boys,' she concluded, 'remember that lots of small changes to our lifestyle make a big change for Planet Earth so keep up the good work.'

Hometime was on the horizon. Like a sheepdog, she herded the pack of rambunctious 6-year-olds towards the tarmacked playground with hop-skip-and-jump squares, climbing apparatus and a sand pit.

'Have a good weekend,' she called, blinking furiously to disperse tears.

Witnessing the hugs and kisses of mothers reunited with their children was always bittersweet. Charlotte knew those women didn't deserve to bear the brunt of her frustration. Suppressing the swell of angry resentment, though, was getting harder. She suspected that not even a smile drawn in permanent marker pen could disguise her sourness as kids produced the daisy chain jewellery made during lunchbreak to delighted parents. Some of whom sported a baby bump to add to their brood.

Charlotte liked to think she was a parent to these schoolkids. But, like Chloe, they didn't satisfy her motherhood cravings because the job was only temporary. She became a part-time parent, a glorified babysitter whose role began and ended with the school bell. At 3.20pm, when they disappeared home, she was hit with empty nest syndrome, a horrible feeling of hollowness as if all her chicks had flown the nest.

You're not meant to be a mother, you're not meant to be a mother, you're not meant to be a mother

For a month, this broken record had haunted Charlotte. Distracting herself, she alphabetised English exams, tidied up reports and bundled pencils and rubbers into her desk drawer. But the vile words rekindled deep-rooted doubts. Was infertility a hint that she would make a terrible parent...?

Charlotte's gaze roamed to a Polaroid at the bottom of her drawer. She'd contradicted school policy by bringing a personal picture onto the premises. It was one of her favourites. Taken a few years ago, John had serenaded her on a gondola in Venice. She couldn't help imagine what their gene pool might create. If a son or daughter would have John's dark colouring, her gingery curls, his stoicism or her clumsiness.

While she gobbled a packet of biscuits, a magpie strutted along the windowsill near a crop of cherry blossom trees. She immediately thought of the children's rhyme – *one for sorrow, two for joy, three for a girl and four for a boy*. But there was no magic number to predict when a baby girl or a baby boy might arrive in her life. If ever.

'Hi, John,' Charlotte said, answering her burring mobile.

'You okay?'

'Yep.'

'You sound tearful?'

'Oh no,' she sniffed, clogging up her sinuses, 'it's just hayfever.'

'Well, I rang the fertility clinic and there was a cancellation so I've managed to fast-track an appointment. It's for next Wednesday. The calendar showed Brooklands Primary has an Inset day so you'll be free.'

'Oh, um...' Charlotte felt ambushed.

'It's daunting, I realise, but it could shed light on our problem.'

My problem, she thought, not *ours*.

'So, you'll put it in your diary?' John pressed for confirmation.

Beyond a year, couples were advised to investigate their failure to conceive. She had kept delaying the consultation with an obstetrician because a doctor would instantly diagnose her endometriosis. Stalling had enjoyed a high success rate until now when her reserve of excuses was empty.

Perhaps the day had come to stop this charade. To stop hankering after the family she'd always envisaged. The wholesome mum in a pinny scattered with baking flour; the dad, the breadwinner, working hard so his family never went homeless or hungry; the cherubic kids.

'No, I won't attend the appointment,' she stated, finally reconciled to ending this deception.

'Why not?'

'Because…'

'Surely the only reason not to go to the clinic would be if you were pregnant?'

'No…'

'Charlotte, is this a convoluted way of telling me that we're going to have a baby?'

'No…'

But then her skin turned the colour of cowardice. Even if she was haemorrhaging hope of having a family, John's resolve hadn't wavered. Lots of couples survived infertility. Maybe they learnt to improvise – employed a surrogate mother, succumbed to IVF, adopted – but she knew those options weren't a substitute. John had fallen in love with fatherhood and would leave her if the truth was broadcast.

His joy transcended the phone line. Tangible, she could taste it, touch it. She had to be cruel to be kind. But she was too kind to be cruel.

'Yes, John,' she took the first step down a slippery slope, 'I'm pregnant.'

CHAPTER 6

Perched on a craggy mountainous peak, *Rutherford Castle* had presided over the Scottish Highlands for centuries and its rural setting enthralled every generation that retreated to the family's 900-year-old country home to escape fast-paced careers in the city.

'Watch out!' Titty cautioned, and her mother swerved to avoid the magnificent peacock roaming its grounds.

'Frightfully sorry,' Maud Wedgewood-Beaverbrook wound down the window to apologise to the bird though she wouldn't hesitate to kill its compatriots during a spot of game shooting.

Collected at Aberdeen Airport, their rental 4x4 squeezed through the portcullis flanked by watchtowers. The castle also hosted an eighteen-hole golf course where Lord Rutherford and snobbish friends in Argyle sweaters teed off while red deer patrolled the boundaries and Roderick's sister unleashed a cracking drive volley on the tennis courts during a lesson with a private coach.

'Hello, darlings,' Lady Philippa Rutherford greeted them as the jeep lurched to a stop beside the self-styled Queen of the Castle.

The actress may have retired from Shakespearean dramas. But she had lost none of her theatrics. Head-to-toe in the family's tartan, she puckered her rouge lips to exchange *mwah! mwah!* kisses and quote the Bard.

'Absence doth sharpen love,' she declared.

'I've missed you more,' Titty flattered the actress.

'Oh, look at my darling daughter-in-law. So beautiful. Shakespeare must have been dreaming of a woman with your bone structure when he created your namesake, Titania, the fairy queen in *A Midsummer Night's Dream*.'

'Ha, I wish I could take the credit.'

'Our flight was unbearable,' Maud moaned, smoothing her grey locks underneath a flat cap.

'Mama and I got stuck with the riff-raff in economy.'

'Yes, we lost our first-class seats to a nervous flier. The crew upgraded him because his symptoms eased in less claustrophobic surroundings. Pathetic chap.'

'Well, it's wonderful you're here,' Lady Philippa swept a silk scarf over her Barbour jacket paired with breeches and riding boots.

The three women bowed, deferentially, to the suits of armour guarding the entrance.

'Worn by heroic Rutherfords in the Battle of England,' she said.

'Yes,' Titty agreed, blowing her fiancé's trumpet, 'and now Roderick is waging his own war against corrupt forces.'

Gordon, the carrot-topped butler, ushered them into the Garden Suite. Lancet windows showcased *Rutherford Castle*'s parterre which backed onto the grass tennis courts maintained to Wimbledon specifications. Dappled in weak sunlight, the formal grounds were meticulously manicured. Crisply-trimmed boxwood hedges created the border. Interspersed by formal statues, box leaf honeysuckle was the gardeners' edging plant of choice; ivies and geraniums used as ground cover; asters provided a splash of mauve flowers, wisteria and white roses climbed the trellis and heavily-scented dianthus was an enchanting touch.

Historic for its royal banquets, the Garden Suite would soon stage its tenth Rutherford wedding reception when Roderick and Titty's ceremony was conducted in the castle chapel. A grandiose black chandelier drew attention to the 11th century barrel-vaulted ceiling. Gilded gold frames exhibited the Rutherford coat of arms; logs forested from the Highlands were ablaze in the open fireplace; Mackintosh tapestries decorated oak-panelled walls and matched the scrolled backrests on Louis XV-throne dining chairs.

'The caterers have prepared a sample buffet,' Lady Philippa began, clicking her fingers to cue an army of kitchen staff.

With military precision, they lined ten different soups along the antique table, a prime example of purplewood and gold marquetry hand-polished with wax lacquer. Each woman tucked a napkin into her shirt and sat, commandingly, like a judge poised to deliver their verdict to cowering auditionees.

'This wild mushroom has a rich, earthy flavour,' Maud commented, tidying her hair with a tortoiseshell barrette.

'Too wintry for a June wedding?' her friend asked.

'Hmm, perhaps.'

'The tomato soup is delicious,' Lady Philippa said.

'Tomatoes are too mundane.'

Lady Philippa swirled her spoon in the next three options.

'Still vegetarian?' she asked Titty without a shred of respect for the decision that impacted the wedding menu.

'Yes,' Titty replied, one area immune to compromise. 'I simply cannot condone killing animals for food when more humane sources provide equal nutrition.'

'The lady doth protest too much, methinks,' Lady Philippa dismissed.

'Yes, she speaks an infinite deal of nothing,' Maud used a criticism from *The Merchant of Venice* to agree her vegetarianism was a bloody nuisance.

'You fool,' Philippa berated the chef for grinding an excess of black pepper over the butternut squash soup that induced a coughing fit.

The sheepish lad glued his eyes to the parquet flooring as if wishing the planks would shift to create a sinkhole that engulfed him.

'Please, Lady Philippa,' he grovelled, aware the consequence of carelessness was immediate dismissal.

'Tis an ill cook that cannot lick his own fingers,' she chucked Shakespeare at him.

'My lass is pregnant...'

'Leave the premises.'

'...and our growing family relies on this income.'

Ruthless, Lady Philippa advanced to tasting the artichoke soup before he collected his coat with a P45 already in the post.

'More delicate,' she appraised.

'Milder, too,' Maud was pensive.

'A neutral starter might be wise.'

'Yes, otherwise one risks eclipsing the main course.'

'Quite right.'

Titty dared to express a conflicting opinion.

'Artichoke is an acquired taste. I prefer the pea and mint. It has a more universal appeal.'

'Darling,' her mother condescended, 'only plebs fail to appreciate artichoke.'

'Actually, Oliver hated artichoke so much that papa worried he was allergic,' Titty's remark hit a nerve. 'He had the symptoms of anaphylactic shock. Itchy skin, wheezing, vomiting. Don't you remember? It was dreadful.'

'Your brother is irrelevant,' Maud snapped. 'Everyone knows he shan't attend the wedding.'

'Unless he makes a miraculous recovery.'

'Oh, Titty, don't be ridiculous.'

'It's possible, mama. I read another article in the British Medical Journal about a lady in London who awoke from a persistent vegetative state after six years with full brain functionality.'

'Your optimism is laughable.'

In silent disbelief, Titty stared at her mother, the woman she would become. Maud shared her horsey features and coltish limbs honed though playing lacrosse for the county as a young girl. Though she'd retired from competition, her mother still exuded the understated elegance of a thoroughbred mare and would have flared her nostrils with anger if anyone suggested she was ready for the knacker's yard.

Titty reconsidered the photos in her father's office. Maud was always standing obediently at his side. She, too, had reached the pinnacle of the medical profession yet she was treated like a plus-one. Did the patriarchal attitude of men like Professor Wedgewood-Beaverbrook or Roderick not upset her mother, Titty wondered, or did she also feel trapped in a loveless relationship, too terrified to break free?

'Roderick says the artichoke is a *spiffing* idea,' his mother returned from a phonecall to her son.

'Decision made,' Maud banged her spoon like an auctioneer's hammer.

'Yes, mama.'

Once more, compliance was the pattern of Titty's life because rebellion led to rejection.

Case in point: this wedding. Dreams of subtracting pretention from the equation or a winter ceremony had been crushed by a desire to please her elders. All her opinions were squashed like worthless gnats. It was Titty's *big day,* but she was reduced to a spare part.

Second case in point: Roderick. It was effectively an arranged marriage of Scottish and English nobility. Lifelong friends, their fathers contrived the meeting at Oxford. Her life read like *Pride & Prejudice* with a modern cast of characters. But sometimes she doubted if Roderick was her romantic hero.

CHAPTER 7

Zoë was glad to spot an emergency defibrillator in a box on the wall. Her heart was soaring, fake-tan streaked by sweat, cheeks so hot that steam billowed. This Cardio Craze had been a baptism of fire into the WAGs' world and she prayed somebody in the fitness studio had a first aid qualification.

'No pain, no gain,' the honed and toned instructor motivated the aerobics class dancing to pulsating music.

Zoë squeezed every drop of encouragement out of the cliché while another lunge punished her leg muscles.

'Excuse me,' she dashed to the toilets as a river of vomit surged up her throat.

Strenuous exercise wasn't the only culprit. She had embarked on a super strict diet to fit the mould of a footballer's wife. For seven days, she had existed on nothing but cabbage soup, partly so she could fit into this size 8 Lycra leotard. Not the best idea before sixty star jumps.

'Everything okay, babe?' Sophie arched a tattooed brow as she returned for tricep dips.

'I must have a sickness bug,' she lied to avoid embarrassment.

'Yeah, you don't look in good health.'

By contrast, the model was serene. Not a long bottle blonde hair out of place from her high ponytail that swished like a horse's mane as she moved. A white crop top showcased her washboard stomach with just a light sheen of sweat. Black yoga pants did not disguise her lean silhouette.

'You've definitely done a high-intensity cardiovascular class before?' she asked.

'Yeah,' Zoë said, another white lie, 'I'm practically a professional.'

'Well, I hope I haven't given you Chardonnay's stomach virus. You know nurseries can be a hotbed for bugs and bacteria.'

'No, it's probably just too much wine,' Zoë fibbed. 'Josh cracked open a bottle last night while we watched a film.'

Sophie froze, horrified, and then caterwauled as if prodded with a hot poker.

'Just a joke,' she reassured.

'Alcohol is liquid calories.'

'You don't drink at all?'

'Not a drop.'

A life without booze was like David without Victoria – unfathomable – but Zoë's will to diet was hardening into iron.

'No pain, no gain,' she repeated, lowering herself onto the spongey mat for sit-ups.

Grunting with effort, *giving up* wasn't in her vocabulary. Especially not with her red carpet debut happening next month. She wanted her breath-taking beauty to make headlines rather than her bingo wings and she feared Josh would grow intolerant of her fatty tyres.

'Congrats, ladies,' the instructor spoke into her microphone. 'We've almost finished.'

Zoë coasted on a wave of relief. But, too sore to stretch, even the warm-down was brutal. She worried that an electric shock would no longer be enough to stabilise her heartbeat.

•

'OMG,' Sophie filtered into the foyer. 'That was, like, so rejuvenating.'

'Mmm…'

'I always feel better after a work-out,' she ferreted in her neon gym bag for a towel.

'Mmm…'

Seriously dehydrated, Zoë regretted not bringing a drink and attacked her friend's flask.

'Oh,' she spat, 'that's not water.'

'I'm on a cucumber detox.'

'How awesome,' Zoë lied.

'Yeah, you can feel the toxins being flushed out.'

'Can I have the recipe?'

'Sure, babe,' Sophie unleashed a megawatt smile before she scribbled the ingredients.

Outlined by pink lip gloss, her dazzlingly white veneers bore no resemblance to real teeth and were more like enamel tombstones. It was concrete proof WAGs preferred artificial to authentic. As did Zoë. She had already booked a consultation with the same A-list orthodontist.

'BTW,' Sophie continued, 'permanent beauty products are essential for gym bunnies.'

'You mean like waterproof mascara?'

'No, like permanent false lashes.'

Until now, Zoë hadn't the funds for these pricey treatments, and was mindful that she looked like a Madam Tussauds waxwork whose face had melted.

'I'll text you the details of my make-up artist.'

'Cool, thanks.'

Stripping to swimwear, they entered the dry heat of the barrel sauna.

'So, how did you snare a serial dater like Josh?' Sophie asked.

'No snaring necessary,' Zoë was guarded.

'Oh, pur-lease, don't pretend it's true love, Zoë. We're the same. Motivated by money.'

'No, Josh and I are soulmates.'

'Spare me the codswallop. I was a 16-year-old masseuse when I snared Pete. I'd already slept with the boss of *Liverpool FC* to get a job in the team's medical quarters. Pete thought my magic hands cured his tight hamstring and enabled him to win the Premier League. It was really down to rest and relaxation, but he proposed straight after the match and I've never looked back.'

Now Zoë speculated that honesty could strengthen their burgeoning friendship.

'I was in *Dolls* nightclub wearing a push-up bra, latex playsuit and 6-inch Jimmy Choos that annihilated my credit rating,' she explained, 'but playing the "independent woman" card was my ace move. Josh reckons my parents are millionaire entrepreneurs so there was no financial incentive to seduce him. My surname's actually Hornby. I used a pseudonym.'

'I grew up on a council estate,' Sophie added.

'Me, too, it was a total shithole.'

'My parents are satisfied with working for the minimum wage, proud of their poverty as if humble roots are a badge of honour.'

'Mine, too. They don't aspire for anything more than Friday night fish-and-chips at the local pub, Primark and bingo in a dilapidated hall where the top prize is a day trip to Blackpool.'

'Yuk, what's the second prize?'

'A *weekend* in Blackpool.'

Sophie laughed.

'You won't tell Josh?' her friend asked, nervously.

'No, course not, all WAGs are impostors married to men dumb enough to fall for their cover story.'

'Thanks, babe.'

'So,' Sophie said, 'I'm guessing Mr and Mrs Hornby won't be at your wedding?'

'No chance.'

As if using her trusty epilator to eliminate unwanted hair, Zoë had savagely plucked her parents out of her life.

'When is the big day?'

'Um…' Zoë paused.

'Don't delay. An engagement ring is no substitute for a marriage certificate and most pre-nups won't be effective until after the vows. The other option is falling pregnant. That guarantees a lifetime of generous child support payments.'

Regretting her complacency, the wannabe WAG heeded the advice.

'Lavinia Lace,' Sophie advised.

'Never heard of her.'

'After winning the Beckhams' contract in 1999, she became the must-have wedding planner. Lavinia doesn't come cheap, obviously, but the woman's a legend. For me, she's on a par with Ghandi or Nelson Mandela. Weddings can cause world wars between couples so her peace-keeping skills are vital.'

'I don't want a wedding planner,' Zoë asserted.

'Are you insane?'

'No.'

'But it's so much hassle.'

'On the contrary,' she yearned to take full control, 'Josh's hopeless at management so he's letting me rule the roost. It's gonna be so much fun.'

'Shit,' Sophie exclaimed, checking her iPad with a moist fingertip. 'Time flies when you're gossiping with friends. I'm needed for a job in Liverpool. The nanny will have to work overtime today.'

'Oh, what a shame.'

'Not really.'

'You must miss them?'

'Not as much as miss my pre-pregnancy body.'

The WAGs giggled.

'My agent has arranged a lads' mag photoshoot,' the model dried off, pneumatic DD implants hardly moving as she jiggled with the towel. 'A slutty Easter bunny spread to coincide with their April edition. The stylist is running late, though, so wardrobe is a mess.'

'*Zoë's Zone* has a range of sexy, springtime outfits,' its proprietor had a sudden brainwave.

'*Zoë's Zone*?'

'Yeah, it's my fashion boutique.'

'You own a boutique?' Sophie was impressed.

'Sure do, and I've even got some rabbit's ears in the store cupboard from a fancy dress party.'

'You're a lifesaver,' the WAG hugged her.

Together, they sprinted to the car park, and Zoë was so revitalised by her acceptance into their rarefied community that she forgot her limbs felt like lead.

CHAPTER 8

If Charlotte harnessed all her brain power, maybe the clock would yield to her wishes. But the time didn't change. She scowled at the *2.32 a.m.* display and rolled over in a disgruntled huff.

'Can't sleep?' John whispered.

'Nope.'

'That's the third night in a row.'

'As if I need reminding.'

Insomnia was penance for her crime. Since the deceit, a guilty conscience had kept her awake. To make matters worse, she blamed it on night-time nausea, common in the first trimester of pregnancy.

'Sorry if I woke you,' she dialled down her irritation.

'No problem, it's good practice for parenthood.'

'Oh, yeah, I suppose.'

As they lay in bed, Charlotte ducked from the chink of light streaming through the linen curtains to conceal her grimace. John had excelled in the role of dad-to-be with alarming alacrity. The library was mined for pregnancy manuals so he could gen up on what to expect when his fiancée was expecting. No doubt his zeal was partly to compensate for missing the milestones during Chloe's development.

'Do you still feel sick?' he was concerned.

'Yep.'

Sick with self-hatred, Charlotte wanted to add, stomach churning.

'Ginger tea might help,' John palmed through a baby bible on the pine nightstand. 'Nausea is worse on an empty stomach. The author emphasises eating small, frequent meals. Bland starches are the best choices so opt for bananas, cereal bars, nuts, dried fruit, bread or crackers.'

'Oh, really,' she wrestled with the patchwork quilt.

'I'll go and get you something.'

Before she could object, John returned with crackers and cheese.

'Vitamins,' he continued reading. 'Pregnant women are recommended to take daily iron tablets and folic acid supplements.'

As she bit into a chunk of cheddar, John rummaged for the *Healthy Diet* sheet he had printed off the internet. Charlotte had three pages foisted upon her. They bullet-pointed the benefits of green leafy vegetables such as spinach, broccoli and Brussels sprouts, peas; chickpeas, brown rice, fortified cereals; five portions of fruit and vegetables a day; starchy foods; protein-rich meat, fish, poultry, eggs, beans, pulses, nuts and oily fish such as salmon, sardines or mackerel. Low-fat dairy. Healthy snacks.

'Lemon and coriander hummus to be served with crudités,' John volunteered his preference. 'I noticed it in Waitrose. I'll buy a pot next time.'

Charlotte was handed a fourth page. This time, *Food and Drink to Be Avoided*. It was capped by cheeses with a white, mouldy rind such as brie and camembert or blue-veined Roquefort. Hence the cheddar. She'd wondered why John had suddenly added it to their shopping list.

'These cheeses could contain listeria,' John informed her.

'What's listeria?'

'It's bacteria that may harm the baby.'

Charlotte read on to find pregnancy placed an embargo on more of her favourites like pâté, raw seafood, shark, swordfish or marlin that contain unsafe levels of mercury, alcohol and excess caffeine.

'I wonder if medication could ease the nausea?' he posited, skimming through the book's index for the relevant page. 'Horatia glowed with health throughout her pregnancy so I don't really know the protocol.'

'Lucky her,' Charlotte growled, bitter, still smarting from her malicious comments.

John didn't notice. Within minutes, he slept soundly. His fiancée did not. Ruffled hair from endless tossing and turning, she tried various counting techniques – backwards from 200, sheep, multiples of 22 – to no avail.

'One, two, three,' she persisted, quietly numbering tassels on a decorative cushion.

Charlotte abandoned the plan at four-hundred-and-thirty-two. As usual, her eyes roamed the bedroom. Sleepless nights meant she knew every nook and cranny of the shabby chic room countrified by pine furniture, ditsy flowers, a wicker laundry basket and a rocking chair. Painted in muted yellows, it was supposed to be restful. Now she threw off the duvet adorned with meadow flowers in another fit of anger.

'Fiddlesticks,' she grumbled.

Too hot then too cold in cotton pyjamas, she propped herself up against the fabric headboard and contemplated her stupidity. A woman could fake a lot of things – fur, laughter, orgasm – but a baby was nowhere on the list. How was she going to fake lactating boobs, ultrasound scans, the linea nigra, cravings, water retention? Not forgetting the million-dollar question. In eight months' time, how was she going to fake labour, birth and a newborn baby?

'Did I nod off?' John stirred.

'Doesn't matter.'

'Charlotte,' he confessed to insecurities that she didn't know existed, 'it was such a relief when you told me about the pregnancy. I was terrified that my age was the problem. It pained me to think I was denying you the chance to be a mother.'

Charlotte tried not to writhe as he caressed her rounded midriff.

'The baby's growing,' he said.

'Um, yes, it is.'

The bulge was food not a foetus. Yesterday, she had baked a mammoth batch of vanilla buttercream cupcakes while she brainstormed strategies. Immaculate conception wasn't viable so Charlotte had to be proactive and hope Lady Luck was kind. If she fell pregnant relatively soon, the dates wouldn't give the game away.

'I love you,' she cooed, cuddling up to him, a desperate attempt at making a baby the old-fashioned way.

'Uh-huh.'

Kissing his cheek with a dusting of greyish stubble, Charlotte loosened the cord of his striped pyjama bottoms.

'Oh, darling,' he said, voice buckling under a yawn, 'not tonight. I've got a lecture at the crack of dawn.'

'So, let's make it a quickie.'

'Charlotte, this might sound crazy, but I'm not comfortable with sex during pregnancy.'

'Why?' she panicked. 'Research has proven it causes no damage to the baby. They don't feel anything.'

'I just find it all a bit icky.'

'So, I have to wear a chastity belt for nine months?'

'It's only the penetration part that disturbs me. We can experiment with the other erogenous zones. It'll be fun.'

Charlotte was poised to protest, but the steady rise and fall of his chest set to the rhythm of sleep suggested the battle would have to be postponed.

CHAPTER 9

Incentivised by banks of photographers, Zoë had dropped a dress size. But the diet was dumped for one night. Her first public appearance demanded to be celebrated with champagne and chocolate.

'Public displays of affection should be illegal,' Titty moaned, shielding her eyes with a clutch bag.

The wannabe WAG was straddling her fiancé on the back seat of the limousine transporting them to a Leicester Square film premier in the West End of London. Opposite, Titty sat bolt upright, hands laced, crossed and slanted knees, a dainty pose refined at her all-girls private boarding school.

Twinkling in the moonlight, their limousine passed the sites lining this stretch of the river Thames that was alive with activity – floating restaurants, cruisers and tourists taking a late-night tour on amphibian vessels. The London Eye was illuminated; Zoë hissed and booed at politicians filing out of the Houses of Parliament; a flashmob of Japanese tourists took selfies outside County Hall and black cabs trundled past Big Ben. Between cracks in buildings, the chauffeur alerted the women to the Gherkin and the tall, utilitarian office blocks of Canary Wharf.

'Rod's dad is a politician,' Zoë retorted, glugging Prosecco from the bottle with nothing else in her system but a tenderstem broccoli, kale and quinoa salad for lunch.

'It's Roderick,' Titty snapped, irked by the informality, 'not Rod.'

'I prefer Roddy.'

'No, it's Roderick.'

'Whatever his poncy name is,' Josh said, 'get his dad to change the law if it upsets you so much.'

'Lord Rutherford has retired from the Westminster front bench and has since been more active in The House of Lords which does not make or break laws. It merely advises. Besides, Lord Rutherford has accompanied his son to Brussels. The European Court of Human Rights head-hunted Roderick for a big case. He's based in the Netherlands until justice is secured.'

'Justice?' Zoë laughed. 'You mean until he gets the result he wants.'

'Roderick cares about the truth.'

'Mmm, the truth according to him.'

Vindictive, Titty turned to the footballer. She thought Josh fitted the bill of gormless male model and hated the stylised tattoos that graffitied his arms and torso. Meaningless black-inked shapes and symbols in the name of fashion. She particularly detested the calligraphic scroll of a past conquest on his wrist.

'Unlike you, Roderick has a *proper* profession.'

'Football is a *proper* profession,' Josh countered. 'It hasn't been amateur since the 1960s.'

'Sacrilege,' she said. 'Football's a hobby, a game.'

'It's a valid career path.'

'Kicking a ball into a net doesn't cure cancer or solve global hunger.'

'It can give kids a chance to break the cycle of poverty...'

'...at the expense of their academic education.'

'Or motivate disaffected youths...'

'...to choose a career that lasts a maximum of fifteen years with no future prospects other than mind-numbing punditry.'

'It teaches leadership, teamwork, camaraderie...'

'...and disgraceful behaviour on-and-off the pitch. Spitting, feigning injuries, womanising. You are appalling role models for impressionable young fans.'

'Football teams require a huge number of staff which creates employment…'

'…for people whose aspirations should exceed working in a canteen or mowing a pitch.'

'And the sale of tickets, memorabilia and ground passes raise money that is redistributed to help the poorest members of society.'

'*Redistributed*,' she teased, 'what a big word for your small brain.'

Josh wreaked revenge by groping his fiancée's increasingly pert posterior. It worked to embarrass the prissy doctor. Her cheeks flushed scarlet. She fiddled with the beaded tulle overlay of her demure cocktail dress.

'Your greedy teammates have money to burn,' Titty ranted, 'but none donate their salary to charity. You'd rather buy lurid sports cars that are criminally fuel inefficient, watches with so many diamonds on the dial that you can't tell the time and holidays in parts of the world you can't even pronounce.'

'We deserve a few luxuries with our hard-earned cash.'

'A doctor or a paramedic or a firefighter works hard for his money. Risks life and limb. Don't pretend the offside rule entails the same degree of effort.'

'Well, you didn't exactly work hard to get the *Dr* prefix,' he turned defence into attack. 'It's the age of political correctness, democracy. Yet nepotism is alive and kicking.'

'I wasn't spared the rigmarole of applying to medical schools,' Titty said, though it was an outright lie.

'Why don't you take that silver spoon out of your mouth?' Josh jeered.

'Not until you take that chip off your shoulder.'

As if the limousine was a classroom of bickering infants, Charlotte diffused the tension with an analogy.

'In theatre, a life can't be saved by one person. It's always a team effort. Just like a football game can't be won by a single player. An individual doctor might cauterise the bleeding. One midfielder might score the winning goal. But it's always due to a sequence of supportive manoeuvres by their colleagues.'

Snubbing any common ground, the pair harrumphed and Titty inadvertently put her friend in the hot seat.

'Not drinking, Charlotte?'

'No,' she wished that she had a genuine reason to join the teetotal tribe.

'More crackers?'

'Yep.'

'Belt on its last notch?'

'Almost.'

Exploiting the confectionery, strawberry truffles and pralines were the bump stretching her floral jersey wrap dress, still not a baby. She heaped the chocolates on top of the crackers John had packed in her handbag. How else could she make cardboard edible? She had two packets to get rid of.

'Can I propose a toast for the mum-to-be?' Titty raised her cordial.

Reacting as if the limousine had knocked a speed bump, Charlotte lurched forward with shock. She was foolish to believe a doctor wouldn't sniff out the supposed symptoms. Or, worryingly, the fact it was a phantom pregnancy.

'I'm only a few weeks gone,' she tried to mitigate this disaster.

'Oh, it's marvellous news,' Titty smiled. 'John and Chloe must be over-the-moon? And you were made to be a mum.'

Charlotte winced.

'More champers,' Zoë ordered, playfully, 'to wet the baby's head.'

Any weird cravings yet?' Josh asked.

'Er, no, not really.'

'Have you considered genetic tests?' Titty took over. 'You'll likely have a nuchal translucency screening to look for Down syndrome and congenital heart defects. Based on your risks, your practitioner may also recommend a non-invasive blood screening that looks for chromosomal abnormalities around week 9 and/or more definitive prenatal tests like chorionic villus sampling or amniocentesis.'

'You're a cardiologist not an obstetrician?' she queried Titty's encyclopaedic knowledge.

'I did a 3-month Obs & Gynae placement. In fact, a contemporary of mine from Oxford, Dr Camilla Lake, has since become a world-class neonatal surgeon with board certifications in both obstetrics and gynaecology and maternal and foetal medicine. She works at a prohibitively-expensive private practice in Harley Street, but I'm sure she'd offer you a discount if I pulled a few strings.'

'It's really not necessary.'

'Only the best for my future godbaby.'

'Ha, ha.'

'You look a bit pale, in fact. Possible anaemia. Make sure you're tested for a haemoglobin deficiency. Anaemia can increase your tiredness and impact your ability to cope with loss of blood when you give birth. Your GP should prescribe iron and folic acid.'

'Okay, thanks.'

'Can we expect a shotgun wedding?' Zoë asked.

'Oh, um, no, John thinks it should take a bit of a back seat until the baby's born,' she explained.

His hesitation suited Charlotte who couldn't contemplate planning a wedding while she was so engrossed in this terrible lie.

'Any ideas for names?'

'Er, no, it's too early.'

'Are you a fan of unique or traditional?'

'Traditional.'

'Stupid question.'

'Mmm, a bit.'

'Bo-ring,' Zoë switched to the film. 'Critics are calling it the greatest Bond of all time. It's got rave reports from the *Guardian*, *Times* and *Independent*.'

Josh ogled the come-hither mounds of flesh in his fiancée's plunging neckline.

'You could be the next Bond girl,' he declared.

'Aww, babe, flattery will get you everywhere,' she said, provocatively twirling her crystal cluster drop earrings.

Of the three women, Zoë looked the least likely to become 007's sophisticated femme fatale. She had poured her curves into a metallic pink bandage dress with skyscraper heels. It made a bold clash against her fiancé's black tuxedo.

'No,' Titty thwarted his attempts to fill her glass. 'I've got surgery tomorrow.'

'Just throw a sickie,' Josh was flippant.

'And fail a patient who's been waiting months for a triple bypass?'

'Work hard, play hard,' Zoë interrupted with another of her dubious mottos.

'Not if you literally have a life in your hands.'

'Spoil sport.'

Sticking to elderflower cordial, uncorrupted Titty reached for the dispenser in the marbled front divide.

'ETA,' the chauffeur announced, 'five minutes.'

Unlike Zoë, Charlotte never courted publicity, but she was grateful for the opportunity to dodge a night of John's questions. And his concern. The pregnancy books made him overanalyse all potential problems.

'It's so exciting,' she grinned, energised by the crowds assembled at the theatre.

Titty loathed the celebrity culture, here to support a friend, but even she wasn't exempt from the buzz on the other side of the limousine's tinted windows.

'Good to go?' the chauffeur parked in a designated spot near the pedestrianised square.

'Yep,' Zoë extracted her pocket mirror for a final check of her make-up.

She unscrewed her mascara wand, dabbed more glitter onto her cleavage bolstered by a push-up bra, held Josh's hand and pouted her lips à la Daffy Duck. Then she confronted flashing cameras, a thousand lights, screaming fans. The media virgin had popped her cherry. And her first time didn't disappoint.

CHAPTER 10

The reception of Cheshire Fertility Clinic had magnolia walls. Unlike teenagers too drunk to use contraception, this was no accident. Magnolia was a deliberately subdued tone to negate the fuming red or sad blue of patients given bad news. A compassionate reception sat behind a curved desk and comfortable, brown leather sofas encircled a coffee table that was a platform for mounds of medical literature and light-hearted magazines for those who needed a distraction from being prodded and poked.

It hadn't changed much from the last time that Charlotte was here, fourteen years ago on the eve of her 18th birthday. She'd been having heavy, painful periods throughout puberty and was sent here for a pelvic ultrasound by her GP which detected the toxic lesions that had blighted her chances of having children.

Until then, Charlotte had never doubted that children were on the cards. She came from a family of breeders – her mum managed four, her brothers had three apiece and so did her sister – and they could have spat out several more litters if they'd wanted. Procreating was in their blood. What they were made to do. It had been an earth-shattering shock to hear that she was the odd one out, the runt, the Upton who might never be a parent.

A secret appointment that coincided with her lunchbreak, Charlotte felt too nervous to sit, as if a hundred butterflies beat their wings against the inside of her stomach. A stomach that was getting bigger by the day. Now she could fit maternity wear, John had invited her to splurge on whatever she wanted for the spring and summer season. She'd traipsed around Mothercare feeling like a criminal, an imposter. But it had given him such pleasure to see her dressing to flatter her bump that she'd shelled out a month's salary on elasticated outfits.

Rocking from one foot to the other, Charlotte gorged on a packet of Jaffa cakes while she waited. She caught the eye of a woman on the opposite sofa. At first glance, she seemed perfectly poised, but Charlotte noticed the streaks on her cheeks from rivulets of tears and her knee that jiggled up and down. A man, presumably her partner, was hovering outside the toilets where he'd probably been given a few back copies of Playboy magazine and asked to deposit a sample of his swimmers.

Like drunks an AA meeting or addicts at a GA meeting, all the female patients in this clinic were in the same boat so there was no judgment. None of Horatia's superiority complex. The woman made an unsolicited confession.

'Polycystic Ovary Syndrome,' she said.

'Endometriosis,' Charlotte was equally candid.

'Have you got any of those cakes to spare?'

'Sorry?'

'It's been a tough morning' the woman explained. 'I fancy something sweet. A Jaffa cake would hit the spot.'

Nodding, Charlotte passed her several of the dark-chocolate coated delights still in their cellophane wrapping.

'Mmm, so good,' she chewed, appreciatively.

'Take the packet.'

'Are you sure?'

'Yes, I've got plenty more in stash.'

'Thank you.'

Wringing her hands sweaty with nerves, Charlotte examined her environs. No matter how manicured the grounds, how ambient the lighting, how spick and span the facility, it would always be tarnished by her horrid diagnosis. But she had chosen to come back. The reason was simple. Over the past year, Charlotte had tried to bludgeon her diagnosis into submission with a battering ram called denial, but knowledge was power. She had googled *Endometriosis* (remembering to erase her browsing history) and found stories of women who had managed to conceive thanks to new technology. But she couldn't rely on testimonials from strangers in Colorado or China's Guangdong Province.

Medicine had come on leaps and bounds in the last fourteen years. Groundbreaking discoveries happened every day. Since then, doctors had performed the first full face transplant, grown a human liver from stem cells, created a bionic eye. Made possible the impossible. Surely the cure for her condition wasn't too far away… although, Charlotte feared, like the end of a rainbow, it would never quite be within her reach, always just the other side of the horizon.

Mr Davis, her original consultant, had retired and Charlotte was summoned to a meet a new doctor. She was decades younger than Charlotte expected, just out of medical school if not nappies. Now she was dogged by worries that fresh-faced Dr Cranford was not sufficiently qualified to help. Then again, she was looking for any excuse not to accept the diagnosis.

More magnolia. In Dr Cranford's office, one wall of shelving was devoted to incalculable obstetrics journals; a cork bulletin board was a collage of Polaroids of grinning and gurgling babies she'd brought into the world; there were graphic diagrams and models of the female reproductive system, a phenomenal feat of engineering that surpassed any manmade construction like iron bridges, aeroplanes or turbine engines. It certainly didn't look like the office of a doctor who hadn't a clue what she was doing.

On the dado pregnancy timeline, Charlotte isolated an eight-week foetus that corresponded with her fictional baby. It was infinitesimal, weighing a mere one gram, but it was progressing at a startling rate. Its spinal cord, bones and intestines were forming; arms and legs had lengthened; knees, elbows, wrists and ankles increasingly defined; brain was developing into two distinct spheres that would determine its personality. When, she groaned, would she be able to experience the magic of nurturing new life.

'Hello, how can I help?' Dr Cranford asked, with calm cadence practised over her brief career.

'I want to have a baby,' Charlotte began, drumming her fingers on the desk with nervy impatience.

'As you're aware, endometriosis lesions have badly impacted your uterus and fallopian tubes,' she located the results of a previous investigation on her slim-line computer screen.

'Yes, but I've read about a laparoscopic procedure to cauterise scar tissue.'

'The damage is too severe in your case for it to significantly increase conception.'

'Then forget about non-invasive procedures. Do it the old-fashioned way. Cut me open and scrape it out.'

'Endometriosis is classified as a *work in progress*. New lesions are constantly forming so surgical removal is not a long-term solution.'

Overwhelmed by an onslaught of tears, Charlotte hiccupped her next question.

'How low are my chances of conceiving?'

'Low.'

'Quite low or very low?'

'Well…' she was trained to present a positive outlook.

'Please don't sugar-coat it, Dr Cranford. I've deluded myself for too long. I need to hear the truth.'

'Very low. However, pregnancy is not the only way to become a parent. Surrogacy and adoption are viable possibilities.'

As Dr Cranford insisted on plying her tearful patient with leaflets and contact numbers and support groups, the ideas pinged off Charlotte as if she was encased in a lead suit. She'd stopped listening. Carrying her child was an integral, indispensable, part of parenthood. She felt barren, broken, bereft. John deserved the truth. Even if he loosened the chastity belt, they would never be parents.

Charlotte vowed to come clean, but John was delivering a lecture on the Ottoman Empire and she had a busy afternoon. He'd texted to say that omega-3 rich salmon was on the menu for tonight. She would tell him over dinner.

Dashing out of the clinic, she drove their new, family-friendly Volvo estate with built-in child boosters that would never be used and arrived just in time for *Brooklands Primary School*'s Easter fair open to mums and dads and the wider community.

An annual tradition, schoolteachers had decamped from the main school building to the playing fields. Cloudy sunshine shone over the Easter-themed stalls designed to raise money for local charities. Mrs Law, the headmistress, sold handmade curios for the home and garden like bunny egg cups, bronze hare and rabbit sculptures frolicking on the artificial grass table runner and teapot cosies crocheted like chicks. Another teacher oversaw the games stalls. Charlotte, of course, was in charge of cakes and she'd gone overboard last night to whip up *egg*stra special treats as a distraction from the forthcoming fertility appointment.

Bedecked with speckled eggs and twigs, Charlotte had strung a garland of bunnies along the stall and baked a mammoth batch of hot cross buns. She'd created cupcakes with a nest of crispy shredded wheat to house the mini-chocolate Easter eggs; fashioned bunnies from marzipan to top a giant carrot cake; surrounded Simnel cake with bunny confetti; stacked salted caramel brownies like Jenga towers and scattered flakes of desiccated coconut onto crunchy white rabbit biscuits.

Charlotte wove a daisy into her plaited pigtails that poked out from a straw bonnet. She'd always loved the spring. Traditionally, Easter symbolised a time of new beginnings, resurrection. It was ironic that she'd never felt so less hopeful.

'Good afternoon,' her sister said, bounding over from a neighbouring stall where she'd participated in a competition to guess the number of chocolate eggs stored in a glass jar.

Only two years apart, they were peas in a pod. Polly's sprawls of freckles on the bridge of her button nose had come out in the sun. Her wild strawberry blonde curls were swirled into a top knot and she wore a cable knit sweater strained by the weight she'd never shed from three pregnancies, gilet, jeans and riding boots caked in mud from clearing out the stables on her farm.

'Fancy a slice of Simnel cake?' Charlotte asked.

'Yes, please,' she dropped a donation into the box, 'I need some energy for the egg-and-spoon race.'

'Then you'd better have a cupcake as well.'

'Don't mind if I do.'

The sisters chuckled.

'I noticed your name wasn't on the runners list this year,' Polly said, collecting a Peter Rabbit party plate.

'No,' she admitted.

'You realise exercise is good for the baby?'

'Yes, I'm just not in the mood.'

'Still feeling nauseous?'

'Yep.'

Charlotte nabbed a hot cross bun before they sold out and swore Polly to secrecy.

'Don't tell John,' she said, 'he's banned excess sugar from my diet.'

Hands sticky from the sweet treats, the sisters watched Polly's children decorate hard-boiled eggs before rolling them down the hill between beds of daffodils towards the car park. Others played Pinned the Carrot on the Rabbit's Mouth. Undeniably, the most popular stall was shaped like a hutch and run by two experts from a local animal sanctuary who allowed children to make furry friends with a variety of rabbits from fuzz-ball English Angoras to Velveteen Lops and Flemish Giants that weighed more than a stone. Their attention was soon transferred to Mr Trout, the PE teacher, who'd dressed up in a bunny costume with long fuzzy ears and a poufy tail made from cotton wool to lead the egg hunt.

'Charlotte,' her sister began, during a rare lull in trade.

'Yes?'

'I've got some exciting news.'

Polly inserted a dramatic pause.

'I'm pregnant.'

Charlotte coughed up her cake, praying it was a misunderstanding. Surely Polly wasn't about to pop out her fourth baby in five years. So highly attuned to pregnancy, it felt like women everywhere were baby-making machines except her. Driving to school, for example, she'd spotted three women breastfeeding at the bus stop, let a heavily pregnant woman waddle over the zebra crossing and found out that her teaching assistant had conceived while on honeymoon.

'Congratulations,' she tried to be civil, 'but I didn't realise you were trying.'

'Oh, no, it was an Easter surprise.'

'Entirely out of the blue?'

'Yes,' Polly said, waving at her 4-year-old daughter who'd won the egg hunt, 'I must have accidentally skipped the pill. Boom. The next day, I felt funny and took a test.'

Hiding her snarl behind a napkin, Charlotte baulked at Polly's casualness. She was more fertile than freshly-hoed farmland. But babies didn't just happen. At least not for mere mortals like her.

'I'm having twins,' Polly revealed, unaware each spoken word dug the knife of unfairness deeper into her sister's heart.

Charlotte had never fallen foul of sibling rivalry, never begrudged their utopian families. She went to their baby showers, birthday parties, agreed to be godmother, helped with babysitting, smiled and said all the right things. But this bitter pill was tough to swallow.

'Our kids are going to be more like siblings than cousins,' Polly grinned, pulling her into a hug.

I wish, Charlotte thought, crying onto her sister's shoulder who mistakenly believed they were tears of joy.

CHAPTER 11

Titty had a dilemma. Lift or stairs. It wasn't difficult to decide. Climbing six flights of concrete steps after her long shift equated to Mount Everest. Even pressing the *12th Floor* button in the congested capsule required maximum effort.

Whereas *CT* was a cacophonous ward of ringing phones, shuffled paperwork and heart monitors, *ICU* was a sound vacuum. Its patients were in a persistent vegetative state (PVS) kept alive only by medical intervention after sustaining severe brain damage. None were capable of communication and lacked perception of external stimuli and the ability to react.

A glutton for disappointment, the doctor checked the visitors' form. No sign of her parents. The entire Wedgewood-Beaverbrook clan had avoided Oliver since his accident as if traumatic brain injuries were contagious. The mere mention of him made them recoil. Still she hunted for their names, proof they had a crumb of compassion, but the line between hope and delusion appeared thinner than a human hair.

'We lost Mrs Blunt,' an *ICU* nurse whispered, as the family stooped with sorrow emerged after withdrawing their mother's life-support.

Titty bowed her head. Their relative had been sown into the fabric of the ward for eight miserable years. Mrs Blunt's death elevated Oliver to the unenviable title of longest resident. It was a nasty reminder of his wretchedly low odds. Fewer than

20% of PVS sufferers improved after a month. The chances of him regaining awareness plummeted as time passed. Now, five years following trauma, recovery was extremely rare and usually involved catastrophic disabilities.

Sensible black courts clacking the floor, she walked to Oliver's room. She knew this ward like neurosurgeons knew the human brain – an intimate understanding of every corridor, connection, compartment – and could have navigated a path in her sleep.

Paintings donated by the hospital's benefactors lined the corridor. Titty paused to admire a replica of The Hay Wain by Constable. Set in Suffolk, oil paints depicted a nostalgic natural world. A farmstead, horse-drawn cart, meandering river, dog, the textured bark of oak trees. Others featured peaceful seascapes and flocks of birds. It was odd, she thought, all the creative and technological strides, and human beings still resorted to the primitive beauty of nature in their hour of need.

'Oliver,' Dr Finnegan spoke to the patient, 'raise your right arm if you can hear my voice.'

From the doorway, Titty watched the neurologist complete his auditory assessment.

'Oliver, raise your right arm if you can hear my voice.'

Still no response. Then Dr Finnegan banged his hands like cymbals. He asked Oliver to blink if he heard the clap.

'Nothing, I'm afraid,' he apologised to Titty.

'Try again.'

'Not now.'

Crestfallen, optimism was difficult, but stubbornness was a Wedgewood-Beaverbrook attribute. It stoked her fire of determination to crack the PVS code and find a cure. Between shifts, she researched cases for any new treatments or tests.

'He'll respond tomorrow,' she asserted.

'Hmm, maybe.'

'No, not maybe, definitely.'

Titty's behaviour towards her brother had evolved over the past four years. Initially, she was scared to speak, touch him, watch a doctor exercise his joints. Time had eroded these inhibitions. Now she allotted several hours each week to recreate their rapport. Obviously, the flow was one-sided, but she cherished any contact.

'Still getting your beauty sleep?' she jibed, kissing his cold cheek which a nurse had shaved.

This evening, she refreshed the mixed freesias on the pine bedside cabinet whose smell provided a sensory stimulus. Titty tried constantly to personalise his hospital room. The swashbuckling action-man had collected a hoard of nautical artefacts from his intrepid explorations and transplanted them from Oliver's inner-city flat to shelves on the insipid walls. Glass bell jars crammed with pebbles that had once studded the Cornish coastline; clumps of seaweed; a two-masted Dutch schooner scale model; a myriad of seashells from Hawaii and Florida with striped ridges, whorls, cones and shark teeth from his gap year in Queensland.

Offering an abundance of maritime charm, Titty hung her navy trench coat worn over a formal square-necked dress on the anchor hook that he had salvaged from the Pacific Ocean floor.

'What a busy week,' she said, plopping onto the chair. 'I did three pacemakers on Monday, spent Tuesday at a medical conference in Bristol, Wednesday and Thursday were manic, and today I assisted with a groundbreaking case of congenital twins. I helped to separate their shared aorta.'

Her brother blinked. Although Roderick called them *zombies*, the lower brain stem in PVS patients was still fully functioning so flickers of life were frequent. But none indicated awareness.

Unlike Titty, Oliver didn't obey their parents' commands or yearn for their respect. Groomed to inherit the throne, he trained as a doctor, but refused to forgo his hobbies like deep-sea diving, quad-biking or dating girls with single-barrelled surnames.

Oliver was brave enough to be the family's black sheep. Hence his surfing trip to Newquay. One February, the seasoned surfer was wiped-out by a freak wave and smashed his head against the rocky seabed. The impact was devastating. A helicopter airlifted him to Bristol, its whirring blades exacerbating the urgency, before Titty flew in from

London to accompany the ambulance relocating him to a special brain injuries unit. Neither her mother nor father, nor her younger twin sisters, came within a 100-mile radius.

Oliver wasn't just her brother. He had been her best friend, ally, confidant. Someone to share the burden of the Wedgewood-Beaverbrook medical dynasty. Titty couldn't abandon him, obliterate his memory, though she kept the visits secret from her parents. A smattering of his buddies from the surf school or rock-climbing club or ex-girlfriends sometimes appeared on the visitors' form, but she was the most frequent visitor bar none.

'Sunday night was special,' she continued, spinning the wooden globe decorated with push pins of Oliver's adventures.

A sudden guttural cry from the Blunts made her shiver. Titty focused on extracting *Gossip* magazine from her taupe Mulberry Bayswater bag. It contained exclusive photos of the James Bond premier which cemented Zoë's celebrity/WAG status.

'She's like the cat that got the cream,' Titty laughed. 'Except now it's a low-fat alternative.'

Ironically, Oliver bore the hallmarks of a real-life Bond. He was a connoisseur of experience and, in sharp contrast with Roderick, suave without being smug. Zoë had fallen head-over-heels for him when she nabbed an invite to his weekend of bungee jumping. The romance wasn't requited and he let her down with dry wit and cool competency just like the iconic spy.

But it was hard, Titty thought, to picture 007 in this sorry state. Ghostly pale, his muscles had withered, mop of limp hair, skin once tanned from his outdoor pursuits now paper-thin and deoxygenated. Nutrition through a feeding tube. Limbs moved regularly so they didn't develop pressure ulcers.

Titty released a yawn. Roderick had just texted to confirm he was staying in Brussels all week. More appealing than an empty flat, she bedded down beside her brother at the hospital which had become a second home. Then she took off her court shoes, folded her coat into a makeshift pillow and dimmed the lights. Oliver smiled. With her last fragments of desperate delusion, Titty told herself a white lie that it was a clue that he valued her company.

CHAPTER 12

Like its owner, *Zoë's Zone* had undergone a range of drastic cosmetic procedures after Sophie suggested a revamp would make the boutique hit the big-time.

'Wow,' its owner gasped, slack-jawed, as she arrived for the evening relaunch wearing a midnight blue lamé jumpsuit, orange patent platform heels and onyx choker.

Sophie, the self-appointed project manager, had banned her friend from visiting the boutique while it was shut for refurbishment. Zoë welcomed any measures to boost profits. No matter how much she loathed its new aesthetic.

'Hello, babes,' she greeted the first guests whose flashy transportation injected style into the suburban street.

Over black wood flooring, the WAGs sashayed to collect a pomegranate mojito mocktail (sans rum) from the angular pay desk while friends of Sophie with geisha face paint modelled eye-wateringly skimpy lingerie.

'Gorgeous,' Tiffany, a former Miss England, inspected the geometric wallpaper.

Creosote-coloured, she defied the chilly temperatures with a chavtastic leopard bralet, black PVC pencil skirt and perspex heels. Tiffany wouldn't have looked incongruous in Amsterdam's Red Light district. Except for the £25,000 crocodile Birkin. Inside the bag, she carried a tiny toffee Maltese poodle, a Maltipoo, who stuck its snout through the handle. He'd been glamourised for the swish soirée with a top hat and black waistcoat.

'Yes, it's a massive improvement,' Sophie blew her own trumpet with inexhaustible enthusiasm. 'The glittery stuff was an eyesore.'

'Bought in a moment of madness,' Zoë lied, a sucker for shimmer and sparkle.

Under new spotlights, the pattern matched the boutique's monochrome minimalism. Pink was out; black was in. Fifty shades of fluffy replaced by faceted crystal and chrome. White Phalaenopsis orchids in silver pots framed a beauty bar; frameless oriental prints of Buddhas and Shih Tzus on black walls papered with interlocking hexagons; chic Bonsai trees planted in vases of black pebbles demarcated the changing cubicles.

'Those feather boas were thrown on the rubbish pile,' Sophie explained, 'but maybe I should have offered them to a fancy dress shop instead.'

The WAGs' cackles boiled Zoë's blood. She chewed her tongue to thwart a tirade of abuse. This boutique used to be her creative outlet. Now her only influence was a lone wall quote.

'Ooh, I love the sculpture,' another glamour model squealed, pointing to a blue and black slate Buddha imported from Tibet next to the chaise longue reupholstered in black leather.

The owner dreaded the price tag. Plus, her expenditure wasn't limited to accessories. *Zoë's Zone* now sold clothes from top fashion houses. It was more Chloé and Cavalli than the crème de la crème of Cheshire's high street designers. But the renovations had achieved a record number of Facebook likes.

'You've got to speculate to accumulate,' she chanted, under her breath, praying the adage was true.

Besides, increased custom and imminent access to Josh's cash would soon be the hydrogen bombs to obliterate her mounting debts. Relations had rocketed in that department. Weeks of unsubtle hints had convinced him to set a date for the wedding. It wasn't the beach event that she'd envisioned since childhood, but a decadent Christmas do could be equally exciting.

'Those pink macaroons belonged in the bin,' Sophie said, unapologetically.

'Yeah, a minute on the lips...' the former Miss England patronised.

'...a lifetime on the hips,' Zoë recited.

Every ingredient of the complimentary nibbles on the pay desk had a prefix – gluten-free, wheat-free, dairy-free, preservative-free, additive-free, sugar-free – so chrome bowls now rattled with superfood nuts, berries and mung beans.

How bizarre, Zoë realised, the rich WAGs aspired to the emaciated figures of women living on the breadline in third world countries. It wasn't even an altruistic stunt in the style of Angelina Jolie who was rake-thin to empathise with starved Africans; it was to conform to a Barbie-esque version of a beautiful body. But she was happy to shell out thousands on empty health foods, to be accused of having more money than sense, so mixed up in this trend to resemble a plastic doll.

'Welcome to *Zoë's Zone*,' she grinned at Margot fresh from a Caribbean cruise to find a new toyboy.

'Holy crap,' the pensioner hesitated, struck dumb by its transformation, dressed in a bandeau crop-top and skirt with costume jewels and black eyeliner to amp-up the attitude.

'Is that a good or bad reaction?'

'Um... it's different.'

Zoë rejected the adjective. Nowadays, different was synonymous with better. But not uttered in this tone. Margot accepted a non-alcoholic cocktail. The tart pomegranate made her gurn. It went back on the tray.

'Any luck in the Caribbean?' she asked, conscious Margot's acrimonious third divorce had burnt a hole in her savings despite Amanda Cassidy's admirable efforts.

'Paul von Borgan, a mega-rich 29-year-old Wall Street trader.'

'If I wasn't happily engaged,' Zoë joked, 'I'd ask if he had a brother.'

'Unfortunately, Paul is balding prematurely,' she said, fickle, 'but he was charmed by the wisdom of an older lady. Apparently, I remind him of the grandmother he adored. I chose to take it as a compliment.'

'Ugh, it reeks of incest,' Sophie was revolted, although chemicals had frozen her forehead so emotions were tough to express.

'Anyway,' Margot persisted, 'he's invited me to holiday on the yacht that he moors in the Cayman Islands so my summer vacation is sorted.'

Despite sharing Zoë's penchant for fluff and frills, Margot was attracted to a black-and-gold jacquard Moschino cocktail dress on a modern mannequin crafted from silver wires with diamonds for eyes.

'It'll be fabulous for my trip to New York. Paul's promised to wine and dine me for a week. Broadway shows, Park Avenue restaurants, Hudson River tours on his private jet. If successful, he might be persuaded to add my name to the deeds of his 5th Avenue apartment.'

'Not if you look like mutton dressed as lamb,' Sophie snorted.

'Yeah,' Tiffany twisted the insulting knife, 'Moschino isn't for women so far past their sell-by.'

'Well,' she stumbled, 'can I at least try it on?'

'Margot, we no longer sell your size,' Zoë regretfully informed her old-age idol.

'Do you know this old lady?' Sophie was repulsed by their possible friendship.

'No, she just keeps hanging around here like a bad smell,' Zoë quickly silenced any doubt.

Rejection from the skin-and-bones club made Margot's eyes glaze with tears. And her tanned skin turn a humiliated red. She reached for a macaroon and, to her dismay, got a mung bean.

'Come back when you've lost half your body weight,' Sophie tormented like a school bully.

'Or when you've found a fashion sense,' Kerry, a beauty technician, goaded.

Turning to leave, Margot's black ankle-strap sandals tripped over the new grey mohair rug. It split her magenta peplum skirt to reveal a lacy thong between buttocks troubled by orange peel. The girl gang sniggered.

'Hi-la-ri-ous,' Sophie held up her phone for a picture.

For the first time, the va va voom pensioner suddenly appeared fragile, fallible, as she squirmed like an upturned insect struggling to regain its balance. Zoë should have extended a helping hand or chastised her friends. But she was too infatuated by fame and fortune to risk upsetting them.

'Funniest thing all year,' she agreed, proposing a group selfie with the OAP that would soon go viral.

CHAPTER 13

'Giant pandas eat for up to 14 hours a day,' Chloe rattled off another fact.

To qualify for the Animal Awareness badge, the Girl Guider had been researching an endangered species.

'Sounds ideal,' Charlotte said.

'Bamboo makes up 99% of their diet.'

'Oh,' her stepmum reconsidered, 'I've changed my mind. Maybe I don't want to be reincarnated as a panda.'

The little girl chuckled, stabbing a sausage with her plastic fork as the trio enjoyed a barbecue on the sun-drenched patio.

Staying indoors was sinful on this glorious June day. Above, the turquoise sky was smattered with nebulous clouds. Leafy apple, plum and greengage trees swayed in the refreshing breeze and insects sung from hiding spots in flora and fauna.

'Save some food for me,' John called, hunting for the blow-up paddling pool in the ramshackle shed.

'Then you'd better be quick,' Charlotte joked.

'Yep,' Chloe slopped homemade tomato sauce onto her hotdog, 'it's delicious.'

Horatia's daughter relished these twice-a-month Saturdays with John when the vegan diet was relaxed.

'Can I water the sedum?' she jumped up.

'Of course, honey.'

Charlotte smiled as the enthusiastic youngster attached a rose to her watering can for the starry yellow sedum crawling over the meandering brick path. It led down to a stream inspected by the globular eyes of a frog floating on a waterlily. Camouflaged with green, brown and yellow blotches, its ribbits were the overture of their afternoon. Kingfishers skimmed over the water hunting for fish. Minnow were in abundance as were newts.

'Want some help with the hosepipe?'

'Nope, I can manage.'

'Good girl.'

The back garden of Chloe's posh townhouse was a deserted concrete yard – John's ex-wife was a stereotypical city dweller who preferred tarmac to turf – and the girl loved helping Charlotte cultivate this cottage garden.

Gifted with green fingers, she made it come alive in summer. A perimeter picket fence was entwined with roses. Lilac wisteria climbed the trellis that cordoned-off the vegetable patch where carrots, onions, radishes proliferated. The grass was left long to provide a safe haven for wildlife. Flowerbeds were strewn with pockets of pastel perennials, cornflowers, poppies, lavender and daisies. Bees swarmed to tuberous dahlia.

'When I grow up,' she decided. 'I want to get married outdoors, not in a stuffy church.'

'Chloe, you're a genius,' John had a lightbulb moment. 'Charlotte, we could host our wedding here in our garden.'

'I thought you didn't like the idea of a shotgun wedding?'

'I've had a change of heart. I want to make our relationship official before the baby's born.'

'No,' Charlotte intervened, panicked, 'we can't afford a big celebration while we're budgeting for the baby.'

'We could keep the costs down if we did it all ourselves. There'd be no venue to hire or caterers or florists.'

'It sounds like a lot of hassle.'

'Not necessarily. We could keep it simple. Horatia insisted on all the trappings and trimmings. I know from personal experience that a fancy wedding doesn't guarantee a happy marriage.'

Charlotte had seen the professional photographs of their posh service at *Claridge's*. She agreed with John's sentiment.

For her, a wedding was an opportunity to proclaim a couple's undying love for one another, not to be the centre of attention. But she couldn't marry a man whose urgency to get hitched was based on a lie. She had resolved to break the news about the phantom pregnancy to John this weekend.

'I'm too nauseous,' she found another excuse. 'I'd rather not vomit over my wedding dress.'

'We could schedule it for July or August. Your sickness might be easier by then.'

'Summer in Britain is notoriously unpredictable. We couldn't rely on any sunshine and I don't want to get married in the pouring rain.'

'Then let's buy a gazebo.'

'I'd rather wait until the baby can play a part in proceedings.'

'Since when?'

'I'm allowed to have a change of heart, too.'

'Just mull it over for a few days.'

'Alright, alright,' she conceded, postponing the argument until an internet search offered a few more reasons why a garden wedding was out of the question.

Chloe redirected the hosepipe towards her father, drenching his check short-sleeved shirt.

'Watch out!' Charlotte warned.

In demented circles, John chased the 9-year-old around the garden. Charlotte clapped. She tried to ignore the pressure of a dual-function padded and push-up bra bought to increase her cup size and create the deep gorge of milk-inflated boobs. Moods were higher than colourful kites soaring above the surrounding fields until the resurrection of a troubling topic.

'Pandas,' Chloe returned to the table, 'are pregnant for 95 to 160 days.'

'Wow, that's roughly half the length of a human gestation,' John calculated while barbecuing corn-on-the-cob with a flame-retardant mitt.

Oh, no, Charlotte thought, another reason not to swap species. A shorter pregnancy gave her less time to concoct a plan. Or a get-out clause.

'More drinks?' she asked, lunging for the empty glasses.

'No,' John intervened, 'don't tire yourself.'

'But I'm fine.'

'I'll get them,' Chloe said. 'It's hot. The baby might be thirsty.'

Flip-flopping over the flagstones, the girl soon emerged with a replacement tray of watermelon coolers in jade green crystal tumblers garnished with mint.

'You've got the fabled pregnancy glow,' John complimented, kissing Charlotte as he fetched an electric pump for the pool.

The mist was sweat. It ran down her back, pooling at the band of her flossy maternity skirt, and the cutlery slipped in her clammy hands. Ill-at-ease, Charlotte sought solace in a beef burger overstuffed with coleslaw.

'Darling,' he chided, 'I've barbecued you a pregnancy-friendly meal packed with lean protein and nutritious veggies.'

Recently, she had faked a craving for spicy foods, and lived to regret it. John finished searing a chicken kebab served with avocado, gherkin and tomato salsa. She couldn't abide hot flavours. But rebuffing his efforts was too suspect.

'Tasty,' she nodded, fanning a mouthful of jalapeño chillies, jealous of Chloe biting into the patty of ground beef in a sesame-seed bun.

'I know it would hit the spot.'

'Yep, you know me so well.'

Ding. Dong.

A raincloud on this summer's day, Horatia rang the bell and marched out to the garden like a harbinger of doom. Charlotte quickly tipped the contents of Chloe's plate onto hers. Horatia would go ballistic if she saw the signs that a morsel of meat had passed Chloe's lips.

'Ugh,' Horatia complained, scowling at the sun, 'isn't this heat awful?'

Then the financier noticed Chloe had changed out of her cover-up cotton dress.

'Are you trying to give her skin cancer?' she barked, deploring the child's bare arms and legs in a flowery romper suit.

'We've avoided the midday sun,' John refuted the stern criticism.

'And applied plenty of sun lotion,' Charlotte defended.

'Neither of which is a substitute for shade.'

'Well,' Chloe declared, off on a tangent, 'this Animal Awareness project has made me want to be a zoologist.'

'Great idea,' John said. 'Working with animals is so rewarding and it can take you all over the world.'

'Nonsense,' Horatia destroyed her ambition in one fell swoop. 'It is injudicious to work with a biologically inferior species. Humans need to interact with humans in order to develop intellectually although I'm convinced some men at work are still in the Neanderthal stage of evolution.'

Tying the straps of her wide-brimmed sunhat in a bow under her chin, Chloe reached for a dollop of Eton mess unlike her stepmother who had to be satisfied with a plain strawberry.

'Desserts are laced with sugar and preservatives and additives,' Horatia scraped it off her plate. 'I don't want her hyperactive. She has a violin concerto at 6 o'clock.'

John sighed.

'Pandas are excellent tree-climbers,' Chloe persisted with rehearsing her nature presentation.

Preoccupied by her phantom pregnancy, Charlotte's concentration ebbed and flowed and she missed the bulk of the speech.

'Darling?' John nudged her.

'Yes, sorry, I'm listening.'

'Chloe wants to see the baby scan.'

'Erm… of course.'

Charlotte had responded to her fiancé's nagging need for a 12-week ultrasound by downloading a template from the internet. Testing her computer skills, she'd superimposed a date stamp and name onto the grainy image.

'I still can't fathom how I missed the appointment,' he racked his brains.

'Don't worry,' Charlotte assuaged. 'It's easily done.'

'But I was sure you booked the 11.30 slot.'

'No, definitely 10.30.'

Deliberately confusing the times was fundamental to her deception.

'Can I keep a copy?' Chloe asked, riveted by her jelly-bean size sibling.

Disagreement would be conspicuous. Reluctant, her stepmum popped the picture into an envelope. Then she threw up a whole tub of potato salad in the shrubbery. It had been eaten while John disappeared to collect the parasol to protect the baby from overheating.

'Did you find out the sex?' Horatia stared daggers at the photo.

'Crikey,' John exclaimed, 'I completely forgot to ask. I was too busy moaning about not being there.'

'Did you hear the heartbeat?' his ex-wife fired questions like bullets.

'Yes,' Charlotte said, 'it's a magical moment.'

'Girl or boy?'

'It was difficult to tell.'

'There was an abnormality?'

'No,' Charlotte flailed.

'Sounds like the sonographer was useless.'

'Not at all.'

'But you didn't press the issue?'

'Not really.'

'Surprises are euphemisms for cop-outs. Forward-planning is prudent. Mothers who spend nine months in ignorance are eschewing valuable time to plan for the new arrival. I found out Chloe's sex at 3 months. It ensured I could employ painters to renovate the nursery, choose names, shortlist girls' schools...'

John adored his little princess, but Charlotte suspected he would treasure a son, and it was an outright opportunity to triumph where Horatia had failed.

'Actually,' Charlotte proclaimed, digging herself an even deeper hole, 'it's a boy.'

CHAPTER 14

Strapped to a stretcher, Ms Taylor was wheeled into the hospital after struggling to breathe during a long-haul flight.

'It's…just...indigestion,' she wheezed.

Dr Titty Wedgewood-Beaverbrook skimmed her vital statistics, increased oxygen flow to her mask and planted a stethoscope on her chest.

'You're experiencing angina,' the doctor diagnosed a more serious complaint.

Encouraged to take methodical deep breaths, Ms Taylor calmed and the paramedics pushed her onto the cardiac ward without a word of thanks from Titty who was mumbling medical jargon as she fussed with the patient's notes.

'Angina usually occurs when the heart is under too much pressure. It can develop after a cardiac arrest as damaged muscles disrupt electrical signals to control the heart's proper rhythm.'

'Well, I was on a plane coming back from Shanghai.'

'I'm guessing you weren't in China for leisure?'

'No, it was a 24-hour thing. I was there to announce the company's bid to annex a Chinese TV channel before a global audience of billons.'

Titty sighed, though she was secretly impressed by her Far Eastern escapades.

'Have you been to any meetings at our rehabilitation centre?' she inquired.

'Nope.'

'You realise it is imperative that somebody with a weak heart avoids stressful situations?'

'I live for my job.'

'That job might kill you.'

'At least I'd die happy.'

Defiant, the patient plugged her ultra-light laptop into the socket. She spritzed her perm curls with extra-firm hairspray, used blush to conceal her post-attack pastiness, and smoothed her crepe shift dress teamed with nude courts and a cropped jacket. All traces of fallibility were gone.

'Please allow me privacy to Skype the CEO of our Zurich HQ,' she ignored Dr Wedgewood-Beaverbrook's protests.

The curtain was tugged open by a nurse.

'This'll help keep the ward cool during the heatwave,' he stationed a fan on the tray table.

'What heatwave?' Titty asked.

'It's 32^0 outside.'

The doctor hadn't left *Liverpool General* in forty-eight hours. Too busy leapfrogging colleagues to realise June was now July. Or the incoming patients had scorched skin as if they'd been on a spit roast. She glanced at the hospital car park. Brits plundered their summer wardrobes at the first ray of sunshine. A heatwave meant there was now a glut of maxi-dresses, tropical prints and red flesh.

'I'm off to Gran Canaria next week,' the nurse chatted, affably, 'but it's a wasted plane ticket. Forecasters say it's due to be sunnier here. Though I suppose you can't really compare a bucket-and-spade day trip to West Kirby Beach overlooking the Irish Sea with a Mediterranean island.'

Annoyed by the gusts of wind dislodging her chignon, Titty wasn't interested in the minutiae of the nurse's holiday.

'Don't you have work to do?' she snapped.

'Sorry, Dr Wedgewood-Beaverbrook, just being polite.'

'Oh, hang on, fetch Ms Taylor a sandwich from the canteen.'

'I can't stop,' the patient protested.

'But I presume your last snack was at Shanghai airport?'

'No, the hotel.'

'Then it's high time you had a decent meal.'

'Doctors should take the hypocritical oath,' Harriet criticised, 'not just the Hippocratic. I bet it's been days since you had more than a banana.'

Reluctantly requesting two egg and watercress sandwiches, Titty allowed Ms Taylor to revise her preparatory notes and scroll through a hefty backlog of e-mails. All of a sudden, the activity stopped. There had been a power cut to her current of energy.

'You're engaged?' she stared at Titty's ring.

'Erm, yes.'

'To whom?'

'Lord Roderick Rutherford.'

In Titty's family, intimacy was outlawed and she was perturbed by the invasion into her personal life.

'Is he a fine fellow?'

'Erm, yes.'

'And does Lord Rutherford not object to his wife-to-be spending more time with her patients than him?'

Ms Taylor had obviously detected the doctor's humongous ambition. It was hard to miss. Akin to a blue whale suddenly swimming up the River Mersey.

'No, he respects my career.'

'My husband and I have the same dynamic.'

'Husband?'

'Yes.'

'I'm confused,' Titty flicked to the blank next-of-kin page.

'Grant P. Taylor.'

'The politician?'

'Defence Minister, to be precise.'

'Why hasn't he visited?'

'My husband's place is in parliament,' the patient clarified. 'Not at my bedside.'

'There's no mention of a spouse in your file,' she queried, 'nor do you wear a wedding band.'

'I don't want to be defined by marital status.'

Me, neither,' Titty stated, recalling a row with Roderick about adopting his surname.

'Guarding national security, sucking up to his constituents, furthering his career and being a dutiful husband is Grant's order of priorities.'

'But didn't a massive heart attack push you to the top of the order?'

'My husband's order is indestructible. Years ago, in 1989, I had a hysterectomy. Grant gave precedence to entertaining German dignitaries on a tour of the UK.'

Titty's instinctive response was horror. It wasn't as if Mr Taylor had prioritised peace-talks with Soviet Germany to presage the fall of the Berlin Wall. Harriet described a blatant attempt at currying favour with international politicians. But a memory blunted her sword of disbelief. When her brother nearly died, Roderick hadn't left Liverpool Crown Court. She had spent that sleepless night at the hospital completely on her own.

'The hysterectomy is why you don't have children?' Titty pried.

'No, Grant considered them an impediment to our career ambitions.'

'My mistake,' she said, stunned Ms Taylor had repeated Roderick's exact rationale for not including kids on their 10-year plan.

'When I was younger, it felt a bitter pill to swallow, but Grant was absolutely right.'

'Mmm...'

'We're lucky,' Harriet avowed. 'Women search their whole lives to find men who don't aspire to spend their lives on the sofa drinking beer and watching football.'

The doctor nodded. She had felt angry Roderick would remain in Brussels for her birthday. But hard-working men deserved support not spite. She would send him a text to apologise.

CHAPTER 15

According to Zoë, altruism was impossible. Selfishness lurked under every good deed. People admired the WAG for organising her fiancé's surprise 30th birthday party. But the real motivation was to guarantee a headline-grabbing bonanza.

'Woohoo!' she exclaimed, shimmying under a limbo stick to cries of *how low, how low, how low can you go.*

Egged on by the cheering crowd, Zoë dipped down until her back crunched. She decided a coconut mocktail was preferable to slipping a disc. The next participant was introduced while she dangled her feet over Rockingham Palace's infinity pool.

'So gorgeous, babe,' she praised, as Sophie struck a sexy pose beside the 8ft inflatable palm tree.

The WAG identified the printed bikini as a *Zoë's Zone* top seller. One of many since the boutique's relaunch. Bombarded by jealousy, she noticed the model's surgically-enhanced assets stretching its tiny triangular cups. She peered down at her pathetically petite version easily contained within the luau flower halter-neck bra. Implants were next on her agenda.

'Best party of the summer,' one reveller screamed.

'Yeah, wet and wild!'

'Awesome!'

Bursting with smug satisfaction, Zoë surveyed her Hawaiian-themed success. Two teams of men – Flamingos vs Parrots – played water polo. Flash, fashionable and fatuous girls rocking Lei headband and bracelets yelped as boys cannonballed into the pool and splashed their designer swimwear. A pair of muscly footballers whacked the beach ball piñata. Others got drunk on tropical cocktails.

'Aloha,' Titty returned from transitioning into a Hawaiian hula girl at her friend's behest.

'Roderick wouldn't recognise you,' Charlotte was stunned.

'Not that I'd pass for a native Pacific Islander,' she said, uncomfortable, rigid as if wire had been threaded through her limbs.

The girls ducked as a squawking blue-and-gold macaw that Zoë had hired for the event flew overhead.

'You should know stress is a killer,' Zoë lectured the doctor, 'and a leading cause of heart problems. Dancing is therapeutic. Enrol in the Taylor Swift school of life and learn to shake it off.'

Titty seized a blue mojito and swayed to Hotel Tropicana. The foil tassels on her hot pink skirt created an electrifying light display. But decorum was quickly reintroduced as her behaviour attracted unwanted attention from footballers in board shorts and beaded wooden jewellery.

The old friends explored the buffet. Charlotte's search for sausage rolls was vain. Carbs were exiled from this buffet. Served on palm leaf platters, it was a fusion of salads, citrus fruit and seafood. One chunk of pineapple wasn't going to help replicate a four-month baby bump. Lacking the courage to expose the pregnancy scam, John et al continued to believe she was a mum-to-be. The more time elapsed, the more complicated this lie became. There were so many symptoms to fake. Tonight, the dress code offered some respite. Charlotte could disguise her figure with a tie-dye kaftan.

'Josh has booked our honeymoon,' Zoë announced, tousling her flowing beach hair.

'Which 5-star resort will you pester?' Titty was intrigued.

'Honolulu. The honeymoon suite is on stilts in the Pacific Ocean. All sorts of water sports are available. The tour operator called it "paradise on earth".'

With the subtlety of a pneumatic drill, reinforcing her dream destination was Zoë's second ulterior motive for this Hawaiian party.

'Well, Jersey will be my island paradise,' Charlotte said, pretending there would be a honeymoon once the ugly truth emerged.

'How boring,' Zoë coughed up her mocktail.

Elbowing her insensitive friend in the ribs, Titty drizzled mint and basil oil dressing over her wheatberry, mixed bean and black barley salad.

'If John's still keen on a summer wedding,' she asked Charlotte, 'won't it be more of a babymoon than a honeymoon?'

'Yes, I suppose so, but we've delayed the wedding for the time being. My dad's got to have a hip replacement and his recovery will be slow. I couldn't get married without him walking me down the aisle.'

Charlotte hated herself for jumping for joy when his operation was rescheduled for July which gave her the perfect excuse to cancel a summer ceremony.

'Titty, what are your honeymoon plans?' she deflected attention.

'By way of a wedding present, Lord and Lady Rutherford have kindly granted us a fortnight at their Antibes villa.'

'But you hated it last time,' Zoë said, rustling her grass skirt with a shimmy to the music.

'Ssh,' Titty demanded, concerned showbiz reporters in the vicinity would somehow leak the reality to her fiancé.

'It's true. You got eaten alive by mosquitos. Then you had a bout of sunstroke.'

'No, the villa is marvellous,' she rewrote history.

Covering her cleavage with a tropical serviette, Titty glanced at the surfboard used to serve drinks in the pool. It was a copy of Oliver's. Horrific recollections of his watery blood staining the board flashed before her eyes.

'Josh's here,' Sophie said, a stage whisper to put the pandemonium on pause.

For a moment, Zoë existed in a fog of confusion. Then she realised Josh, the birthday boy, was home after his match. A couple of lads hoisted the holographic personalised banner above the pool. In silence, the partygoers heard him kick off his muddy football boots and manifest at the bi-fold doors.

'Happy 30th birthday!' they yelled.

Josh hardly looked up.

'Fucking goalie,' he ranted, hurling his kit bag against the wall so its entire contents were ejected. 'How could he miss that penalty? The man's a liability. He deserves to be sacked.'

Mortified, Zoë had to intervene if she stood a chance of salvaging this disaster.

'Babe,' she approached, tentatively, as if he was a bomb that a single misjudged comment could detonate. 'I've thrown you a party. All our friends are here.'

But the footballer didn't explode. There were no fireworks. Like the party, his anger just fizzled out.

'I'm going to bed,' he sloped upstairs.

CHAPTER 16

Charlotte pinched her arm. It still didn't seem plausible. Horatia, the woman with zero tolerance of children, had voluntarily joined her baby shopping expedition. Charlotte was powerless to refuse. Suggesting this trip to John had simply been to butter him up after the disappointment of delaying the wedding. She never intended to actually go shopping. But then Horatia jumped on the bandwagon and now she found herself in a department packed to the rafters with baby gear.

'Allow me,' John's ex-wife said, gallantly carrying the weightiest items. 'Lifting heavy loads can increase your risk of miscarriage.'

Laden with newborn apparel, they queued at the John Lewis pay desk behind a woman with a week-old baby curled over her shoulder like a koala. The bub opened a wrinkly eye. It seemed to stare into Charlotte's deceitful soul. The intensity made her shudder.

'What a productive session,' Horatia reflected on their morning, 'we've bought half the shop.'

'Yes, we must have finished,' Charlotte hoped, sweltering in a polka dot blouse, maternity leggings and sandals.

'Not quite,' Horatia revealed, brandishing a hand-written laminated list and tapping the *Nursery Apparatus* section.

Charlotte stepped onto the escalator in Horatia's trail for a torturous hour spent comparing cots.

•

The in-store café smouldered in a subterranean darkness as clouds the colour of concrete and bloated by rain gathered over the Liverpool Waterfront.

'Looks like a storm is brewing,' Horatia predicted a dramatic end to the heatwave.

'Yes,' Charlotte agreed, joining the queue of weary shoppers making a pit stop to refuel on caffeine and calories.

Today's special – crumbly raisin bran muffins with grated pear and tangy buttermilk – was exhibited in wicker baskets crammed with appliances. On the shelf below, a row of bowls were filled with fresh fruit, drizzles and nuts to jazz up smoothies. Triple-tiered cake stands flaunted the smorgasbord of desserts. Banana and passionfruit cake; fruity muffins; lemon meringue taken to a new level with caramel-infused sponge; Cherry Bakewells, a popular stalwart.

'I'll have a frappuccino,' Charlotte ordered.

'Pregnant women should cut down on caffeine,' Horatia dampened her enthusiasm.

'Of course,' Charlotte faltered. 'Water and a blueberry muffin, then.'

'Tut tut, you know fatty foods can lead to gestational diabetes.'

'Alright, just a banana,' she respected Horatia's advice.

The caustic remark echoed one that still rattled her. You're not meant to be a mother. But perhaps these pearls of wisdom were designed to make amends. She magnanimously decided to forgive and forget, always advocating to the schoolchildren after a playground quarrel that forgiveness was the greatest weapon in anyone's arsenal.

'Chloe mentioned you're still very nauseous,' his ex-wife said, pushing the new wicker Moses basket under their table.

'Um… yes.'

'It's unusual for it to persist beyond the first trimester.'

Charlotte nodded.

'Might it be Hyperemesis Gravidarum?'

'Um…'

'Extreme morning sickness. It affects only 1% of women. Kate Middleton suffered.'

'Oh, I remember,' she pretended. 'Don't worry. It's not too debilitating.'

Horatia's metabolism, like her lifestyle, was abnormally efficient. But the sinewy physique clad in a Breton-striped top and tapered trouser was not conducive with calories. Scoffing her slice of vegan walnut cake in front of Charlotte who had to get excited about an unripe banana meant she could have taught Christian Grey a thing or two about sadism.

'Any ideas for baby names?'

'Um, no, not really.'

'How about Balthasar?' she asked, now stirring her frothy cappuccino with a milk-substitute that made Charlotte drool.

'Balthasar…' the suggestion appeared wildly random.

'Yes, he was one of the biblical Three Kings so it's befitting of a Christmas baby.'

'Oh, right,' Charlotte said, unable to fault the logic as she had set the due date for December 19th.

'How about Joseph?'

'Maybe.'

'Or Gabriel?'

A clap of thunder made them jump. Then a bolt of lightning fissured the violent, churning purple sky. Charlotte observed workers take a hurried final puff of their cigarette and race back into the office buildings edging this network of historic docks and canals.

'Chloe showed me the ultrasound scan,' Horatia went on, spectacles perched on the tip of her pointy nose, 'and I noticed something odd.'

Charlotte's jaw locked with tension.

'Odd?' she repeated, trying to adopt an insouciant air, though her heart rate quadrupled.

'Yes, the authenticity watermark is from Boston General Hospital.'

'It's better-equipped for 3-month scans,' Charlotte quickly excused travelling an extra hundred miles while slapping her thigh for not noticing the discrepancy.

'Well, it is a world-leading maternity hospital...' Horatia supposed.

'Precisely.'

'…but it's in Boston, Massachusetts, not Lincolnshire.'

Outside, a sudden deluge of fat globules of heavy rain pelted the Waterfront, distending the tourist attractions along this stretch of the river until they appeared like squat, scale models. Tourists disembarking boats at the Princes Dock Cruise Terminal fumbled to retrace their steps. People exploiting the balmy temperatures on hotel balconies and restaurant terraces regretted not packing anoraks. The scene inside was no calmer. Charlotte had been rumbled. Frantic, she headed for the café's exit. A full foot her superior in espadrille wedges, Horatia easily blocked her path.

'You can run,' she said, wagging a condescending finger, 'but you can't hide.'

Denial was futile. Charged with fraud, Charlotte concentrated on her defence plea. It was perhaps the first token of honesty since falsifying the pregnancy test.

'I never meant to hurt anyone,' she began. 'I suffer with endometriosis. I couldn't conceive.'

Horatia was a hostile judge.

'Spare me the amateur dramatics.'

'Please don't tell them,' Charlotte sank to her knees, startling fellow diners with the show of indignity.

In the midst of appealing for a lesser sentence, she divined Horatia thrived on control, not moral justice. This shopping trip was carefully constructed to inflict maximum damage. Fuck forgiveness. She stood to hear the bail conditions.

'For starters, I need you to convince Chloe to give up the Girl Guides,' Horatia crossed her arms.

'She's a child,' Charlotte refused. 'Not a bargaining chip.'

'Last week, Chloe saved all her pocket money to buy the baby a teddy bear. Her next expense is a cot mobile. Don't you dare take the moral high ground with me. This mess is of your making not mine.'

Charlotte heard her heart break.

'For reasons I cannot fathom,' Horatia said, 'Chloe listens to you, she likes you, she takes your advice on board. She has a Girl Guides meeting tomorrow. You have the power to make sure it's her last.'

CHAPTER 17

All morning, Titty had radiated confidence. Then, moments ago, Professor Wedgewood-Beaverbrook had paged her to his office and warned his daughter to fight all her natural impulses – "be relaxed not robotic, assured not assertive, vocal not vociferous" – to become a more endearing candidate. Now she was plunged into a tailspin of confusion.

'Last-minute nerves?' Richard Lam harassed his rival as they waited outside the interview room.

'No,' Titty snapped. 'You're the underdog. You ought to be popping anti-anxiety medication not me.'

'Eh contraire,' Dr Lam teased, 'everyone loves an underdog and I'm not burdened with expectation.'

'I'd still rather be the favourite.'

'You're forgetting the front-runner often falls at the final hurdle.'

'Then I'll be the exception to the rule.'

'What about the story of the hare and the tortoise?'

To stop jiggling the bow of her blouse, Titty sat on her hands, but then she fretted about her outfit. A stark white blouse, navy blazer and courts. It screamed uptight bitch not kind and caring doctor. Darn it, there wasn't time to change.

'Good luck,' Richard called, insincerely, as she was beckoned by the bigwigs.

In spite of her fighting talk, Titty's radar recognised Dr Lam was a serious threat. He had the one attribute that she lacked.

Different people called it different things, but it boiled down to the common touch, bedside manner, likability factor.

Plus, if it was a politically correct appraisal panel, Richard's working-class background/state school education/saddled with student loans profile could work to his advantage. Posh totties like Titty were the one minority group that society allowed to be discriminated against. But Professor Wedgewood-Beaverbrook was in cahoots with the chairman, allies since those ungraduated years at Oxford, and Titty trusted he would convince colleagues to promote her.

'Good morning,' she greeted the emeritus panel who would determine her suitability for consultant.

The interview room was austere. Off-white walls, utilitarian furniture, slatted blinds, a potted cactus beneath the flip board. It was prickly like the panel of governors, doctors and a departmental matron.

'Dr Titania Wedgewood-Beaverbrook, tell us why you chose a medical career?' Mr Chapman asked, interrogating her through a monocle that magnified his pupil to scary proportions.

'To protect and preserve human life,' she gave the requisite answer.

Titty had vetoed honesty. Pleasing her parents, impressing her fiancé and earning a solid income were not attractive answers. Though Mr Chapman surely knew she was lying enough to look like Pinocchio's sister.

'The hospital's CEO considers you a credit to the cardiology team,' the chairman read his reference.

'Yes, sir.'

'Though I notice the shortage of praise from your peers,' the departmental matron was suspicious.

Despite being a social pariah since medical school, Titty was a tad disappointed not one doctor or nurse had supported her application. They didn't realise her confidence was like limestone – easily eroded – and crumbled behind closed doors.

'The Wedgewood-Beaverbrook family's medical pedigree certainly bodes well for your future,' Mr Chapman said.

'Yes, sir,' she tried to keep calm, 'I sincerely hope that I'm destined for the highest echelons of this profession.'

'However,' the Clinical Director interjected, 'your age concerns me.'

'Youth is a blessing not a curse,' she quoted Professor Wedgewood-Beaverbrook. 'I have the energy, enthusiasm and eagerness that may be absent from disillusioned older candidates.'

'I notice experience is not one of your alliterative qualities.'

Damn, she muttered, incensed by the blunder.

'Actually, my parents, the Professors Wedgewood-Beaverbrook, nurtured my medical education from a very young age so I have a precocious amount of experience.'

Though she was armed with endlessly-rehearsed answers, Titty coughed to clear the lump of anxiety harder than a marble as she name-dropped to justify the promotion.

'I have an excellent academic record with a particular talent for assimilating new information,' she moved on.

'Speak up, please, Dr Wedgewood-Beaverbrook.'

'Um, sorry, this skill facilitated my participation in the Rooks case.'

'Yes,' Mr Chapman referred to his notes. 'Dr Riordan elevated you to lead surgeon though it was your first year of specialised training.'

'Correct, sir.'

Titty's shaky knee suddenly slammed the table. It toppled the jug of mineral water. Litres of liquid and a slice of lemon splashed the Clinical Director's blouse.

'Oh, good gracious,' she rushed to help.

A stern glare suggested she was making matters worse.

'Moving on,' the woman said.

Titty segued into further accolades.

'Aged 28, I was crowned Outstanding Cardiothoracic Registrar of the Year by the Royal Society of Medicine. Two articles I penned – Survival of the Surgeon and Matters of the Heart – were published in the British Medical Journal. I presented at the UK's national cardiology convention last autumn.'

Remembering consultants required more than qualifications, Titty addressed her faux pas.

'I am equally devoted to providing emotional care for my patients,' her nose elongated.

'Hmm,' the departmental matron leafed through her papers. 'Testimonials from past patients seem to be missing.'

'Ray Nixon, 42, arrhythmia,' she alerted them to the solitary entry who'd developed a fetish for formidable females.

'How would you plan and manage a new service?' the Clinical Director asked.

'When planning the new service, I would assess how it fits into the trust both physically and fiscally. I would gather comments and criticism from patients and colleagues and use the data to appraise the advantages and disadvantages. I would ensure the new service was effective and efficient but, above all, safe.'

'Some consultants avoid difficult decisions for fear of criticism from their subordinates,' Mr Chapman commented. 'The Britton debacle indicates unpopularity is not a problem for you.'

Last year, she gained notoriety as the snitch when a peer arrived drunk for his shift.

'My primary concern was patient welfare,' Titty explained the rationale for telling tales to the General Medical Council though kudos from senior staff was the overwhelming motivation.

'I believe fellow registrars subjected you to a hate campaign,' the Clinical Director said.

'Yes, they considered it disloyal.'

'And Dr Britton?'

'After receiving a 2-year ban, he circulated a derogatory e-mail about me.'

'Despite the benefits of being thick-skinned,' Mr Chapman said, 'would you describe yourself as a team player?'

Titty's nose grew to a record length.

'Certainly, sir. I'm a good listener and value different perspectives. I'm empathic, a good communicator and an excellent role model. I respect the contributions and expertise of all staff members.'

'Do you possess any faults?' the departmental matron posed a trick question.

'I work too hard,' Titty fell into the trap.

'Tiredness costs lives.'

'Er, yes, madam.'

Titty had mistakenly believed it was a foolproof answer. Like a fireman saying he was too brave. Or a student too thirsty for knowledge. She backpedalled to repair the damage.

'Establishing a work-life balance is critical,' she said, gesturing to her emerald-cut diamond.

'You're engaged to be married?'

'Yes, madam.'

In eerie silence, the panel digested her response and sent her into a nervous tiz. She longed for the water jug to be replenished. Being put under the microscope was thirsty work.

CHAPTER 18

```
ROCKINGHAM POOL PARTY
SINKS QUICKER
THAN TITANIC
```

Time healed all wounds. Zoë begged to differ with conventional wisdom. A month since the party, bruises still mottled her body from tip to toe and rereading the hurtful headlines that had accosted her Facebook page and Twitter feed didn't help.

The ordeal, however, had taught her one important lesson. Footballers were great if they won; grumpy if they lost. WAGs lived at the mercy of their moods. Failing to qualify for the Europa league next season meant Josh was a misery guts. He skulked off to training without a goodbye, cancelled their St Tropez trip and gave Zoë grief if she moaned at his grisliness.

Unlike her new £30,000 veneers, the shine of this lifestyle had started to fade, but not enough to make slumming it in *Zoë's Zone* store room a more attractive bet.

Pummelled black and blue, the party wasn't the only source of her bruises. Zoë had developed romantic feelings for Josh. So getting the cold shoulder was doubly difficult.

The feelings upset her cold-hearted Venus Fly Trap plan – lure him in, suck him dry, spit him out – and she fought the metamorphosis of lust into love with black-belt karate kicks. A month of Josh's foul mood should have destroyed them. But abstinence, not just absence, made her heart grow fonder and Zoë prayed that she wasn't next on his rubbish pile of exes.

Rumour had it the remedy for heartbreak and humiliation was chocolate. Lots and lots of it. But she had subscribed to a new fad, the baby food diet, promoted by WAGs to create a calorie deficit. None of the 16 jars in Rockingham Palace's kitchen cupboards contained a single ounce of cocoa.

'Forest fruits or mango mayhem?' she debated two breakfast options while Barbara cleaned the floor.

Either way, Zoë realised, the latest elixir of youth was puréed mush. She stuck her spoon into the first tasteless jar of the day. Her slender reflection in the gloss units proved she was beating the bulge. But daily workouts made every muscle ache and this type of exercise didn't stimulate the happy hormones.

'Ooh, aah, ooh, aah,' she raised the spoon to her mouth.

'Can I help?' Barbara asked, though she had little concern for her slave driver in a silk Missoni tribal printed maxi-dress.

'Ring the massage parlour when you've finished cleaning. I need a heated coconut poultice massage and nourishing wrap.'

'Your wish is command, Ms Fraser.'

Irritated by the sarcasm, Zoë tipped mashed raspberries onto the tiles and smudged them with her jewelled gladiator sandals.

'Oops, Barbara, you've missed a bit,' she pointed, casually buffering her nails while the maid worked like a slave.

On her hands and knees, Barbara mopped it up. Zoë deliberately dropped another spoonful. Barbara wiped it away. After ten minutes, Zoë bored of the vindictive game.

'Yuk, yuk, yuk,' she groaned, swallowing a mound of mulch that she tried to imagine was melted chocolate.

The blend of berries failed to fill the famine left by her 6 a.m. gym session. Disparaged, she logged onto Facebook. More malicious comments from trolls making fun of the #partypooper. But Sophie's page featured a new post littered with emojis that was trending nationwide.

'Hashtag: what the hell is this wrinkly wearing?' Zoë read its title.

Curious, she scrolled down. The picture of Margot in her red thong was manipulated into an avatar. Sophie had added lots of degrading speech bubbles. And she'd made memes of other OAPs who used to frequent her boutique. Add a comment, her cursor hovered over the text box. Zoë was tempted to flag it as inappropriate and report it to officials. But, instead, her comment bowed down to Sophie's brilliance.

@sosophie OMG ur so right! #pastherprime #partypooper

Beep. Beep.
Zoë slid off the stool to answer the intercom. Delivery for Ms Fraser. Throbbing thighs meant she crawled toddler-esque to the front door.
'Special occasion?' the chirpy courier asked, presenting a bouquet of lustrous lilac and cerise orchid, germini and roses and a gift box.
'Another nasty offering from tabloid journalists,' Zoë raced to conclusions. 'There's probably a toy Titanic hidden in the flowers. Or a plaque for World's Worst Surprise Party.'
But she opened the box's lid to discover a spectacular Tiffany 18k gold necklace – one heart pendant engraved with her initials, *ZF*, the other with *JR* – and a note.

Sorry, babe. J xx
P.S. Enjoy the necklace
P.P.S. I've booked a weekend in Rome. Pack your bags, we're leaving tonight

Time didn't heal all wounds. Jewellery did. Zoë felt reborn. She thanked the courier and, energised, sprinted to the kitchen to dive into the pot of forest fruits. She had to be in sublime shape for the wedding because it was back on with a bang.

CHAPTER 19

Part of *Brooklands School*'s anti-bulling campaign, this autumn term begun with a pastoral lesson.

'What is bulling?' Charlotte asked, writing the hateful adverb on the whiteboard.

Faster than a rocket launched into space, hands shot upwards from children vying for Miss Charlotte's attention, but it was a rhetorical question.

'Bulling is when a person forces you to obey their instructions,' she underlined.

'Like if my dad makes me clean our car?' a boy wondered, folding his homework sheet into a paper plane, a skill learnt over the summer holidays.

'Not exactly. Your dad's request is reasonable. Bullies often force you to do nasty things. They might threaten, intimidate or scare you.'

Charlotte grabbed a blue marker to distinguish the advice section for victims of bullying on school premises.

'Tell a teacher,' she began, 'even if the bully says no. Bullies act tough. But they're actually weak. They control us to look big and strong because they feel small and vulnerable.'

Charlotte felt stung by her double standards. She had a responsibility to practise what she preached. There was no excuse for Horatia's bullying. She had already ruined Chloe's summer. Due to her distortion of the dates, the girl had missed an action-packed Girl Guides weekend to the Peak District and felt too demoralised to go to subsequent meetings. The void was filled by chess club which made her thoroughly miserable.

'Miss Charlotte?' a little boy called.

'Yes, Thomas.'

'Are you having a baby?'

Charlotte dropped the marker pen. She'd hoped the children wouldn't find out about the phantom pregnancy. She didn't want such good and innocent young lives to be sullied by this dirty, stinking lie.

'Maybe Miss Charlotte's just eaten too many cupcakes,' a cheeky little girl risked a reprimand.

Charlotte's rampant binging had put on two stone. But not necessarily in the right places. A pear, it languished on her hips and thighs so a loose-fitting linen shirt was essential with her denim maternity skirt.

'No,' Thomas was adamant, 'my mummy saw Miss Charlotte buying baby clothes.'

'My mummy's pregnant, too,' Dana, a chatterbox in the back row, announced.

'How lovely,' Charlotte said.

'Her tummy's much bigger than yours.'

'Well,' she concocted a credible reply, 'all babies grow at slightly different rates.'

Ding. Dong.

'Quietly,' she shushed a stampede of 6-year-olds.

Eager to compare seashells and sandcastles and stories of sunny holidays, the kids responded to the break-time bell by racing out to the playground and the classroom emptied so she had twenty minutes to confront Horatia.

'Got a minute?' a Year 1 assistant poked her head around the door awash with times tables and days of the week posters.

'Not really.'

'Pretty please.'

'Okay,' she acquiesced.

Charlotte was unexpectedly frogmarched to the spacious staff room. It was commandeered by a crowd of smiley teachers wearing cone hats who'd gathered under a *Good Luck!* banner. Her arrival initiated a round of applause.

'We'll miss you,' Mrs Law said, leaving a strawberry-red lipstick outline on her cheek.

'Miss me?'

'Yes, but John told us you're keen to put feet your up. Get some R&R. Pregnancy is the perfect excuse for a spot of pampering.'

Dumbfounded, Charlotte wordlessly accepted a glass of cordial from the head-teacher. Mrs Law had tamed her frizzy hair into a bun, hung her thick-rimmed glasses on a chain and worn a smart beige trouser-suit for the party. Adored by parents and pupils, she was a modern-day saint who never made a fuss or let power go to her head. Charlotte idolised her. She was a dedicated teacher with a thirty-year history of fostering hundreds of needy children at her home.

'And taking maternity leave at the six-month mark is a wise decision,' Mr Lark confirmed. 'I remember when my wife had our first child. She regretted leaving it to the last minute to stop work.'

'Yes, six months gives you plenty of time to prepare for motherhood,' Miss Holland's voice was muffled by a mini pork cocktail sausage.

'Though parting is such sweet sorrow,' an English teacher quoted Shakespeare.

Charlotte gawped, quizzically, at the colourful party streamers strewn over the tea and coffee machine, variety of nibbles on the breakfast bar in the kitchenette and balloons tied to chair legs before realising it was a leaving-do. John had coerced her into agreeing to a hiatus at the October half-term. But he must have liaised with Mrs Law to bring it forward. She staggered onto the sofa.

'Aww, baby must be asleep,' the headmistress said, with her hand on the inactive bump.

'Look, Charlotte,' Miss Holland pointed to the cubby hole next to framed "Outstanding" Ofsted reports that was overspilling with congratulations cards.

This outpouring of goodwill from colleagues and children made her tremble with emotion and compounded the horror that her web of lies had spiralled out of control. Enmeshed in its ropes of spidery silk, these innocent well-wishers did not deserve to be gobbled up by the truth if it entered the public domain.

'Ready to cut the cake?' Mrs Law asked.

'Um…' she hesitated.

Celebration swirls of chocolate ganache had never been so unappetising.

'Wow, the baby's stolen your sweet tooth,' the head-teacher laughed.

'No,' Charlotte coughed, seizing the knife, 'just a bit of indigestion. Plates at the ready. Who wants the first slice?'

CHAPTER 20

'Let me in,' Titty demanded, parking her maroon Audi hatchback beside *Rockingham Palace*'s intercom.

'No, it's late,' Josh used his bedroom device, 'I've got a match tomorrow.'

'If you don't let me in,' she threatened, 'I'm going to climb over the fence and key your convertible.'

Groggy, Josh rolled out of bed and lurched for a button to open the automatic gates.

'Have you forgotten to take your anti-psychotic pills?' he exclaimed, jolted awake by the trespasser barging into the dark hallway.

'Don't play innocent,' she barked, 'it insults my intelligence and kills off your single brain cell.'

'Are all doctors raving lunatics?' Josh followed her into the kitchen with his hands in the pockets of his flannel tracksuit bottoms, worn low to expose the Calvin Klein band of his Y-fronts.

'I'm not the crazy one,' Titty didn't mince her words. 'We both know Zoë's in hospital because of you.'

'Fucking hell. Was it a car accident? She can be wild on the roads.'

'There's nothing accidental about cosmetic surgery.'

It still didn't compute. Titty showed him the text received an hour ago while she was operating on a man with a stab wound to the heart. Zoë had deliberately sent the text only minutes before her theatre slot so Titty could not intervene.

'You pressured Zoë into pumping her breasts full of silicone,' she accused.

'Boob implants?'

'As if you didn't know.'

'I thought she was in Majorca for a week's holiday.'

'Did you drive her to the airport?'

'No, she called a cab, but £3,500 was debited from my account and I watched her pack a suitcase.'

'For the ward,' the doctor deduced, 'not warm weather.'

Titty now guessed bigger boobs were his belated birthday surprise. But she offered no apology. Not to a man who forced women to emulate blow-up sex dolls.

'I didn't endorse the procedure,' Josh swore, arms folded across his white crew neck t-shirt.

'Yeah, right.'

'Don't be so glib. I lost my mum to breast cancer. I have 100% respect for women's bodies.'

The confession brokered a temporary ceasefire in their class war.

'Want a drink?' he said, unscrewing a bottle of gin from the latticed metal rack.

Poised to give a sermon on alcohol abuse, Titty's moral compass suddenly veered off track.

'Yes,' she held out a glass. 'Make it a double.'

•

The nurse dropped her diamond earrings, Tiffany necklace and engagement ring into a clear plastic bag.

'Careful,' Zoë warned. 'If anything happens to those stones, I'll hold you personally responsible. And I'll sue the clinic for theft and/or property damage.'

Separation from her jewellery, her material babies, caused intense pain. As did returning to her natural pasty state due to the pre-surgery make-up ban and the baggy hospital gown that was far from flattering. But this private clinic was Sophie's recommendation and, dismissing her wobble as a storm in a bra cup, she proceeded.

'Ready to go?' Dr Shiraz asked.

'Yes, I can't wait.'

'As discussed, the operation will take roughly 60 minutes.'

'Worth every second.'

'Good,' he smiled, pound signs flashing as he authenticated the consent form.

The nurse slackened the bed's brake. Wheeled into the operating room, Zoë's buoyancy was capsized. Glary lights, ominous instruments, latex gloves. Medics dehumanised by scrubs, caps and masks. The smell of bleach to cover blood shed by past patients. All this aggravation for a DD-cup. But she refused to kowtow to fear.

'Just relax,' the anaesthetist injected a cocktail of sedatives into her bloodstream.

•

'Not once?'

'No.'

'Not a single time?'

'No, it's too traumatising,' Titty said, defending her parents, 'and Roderick has more pressing commitments.'

'Hold on, Rod's never visited your brother, either?'

'Like I said, his legal cases can be all-consuming.'

Drink in hand, Josh downed another shot.

'I'm no martyr,' he asserted, 'but I sacrificed the Champions League final to be with mum for her diagnosis and Dad attended every chemo session until the bitter end.'

'Maybe a parent-child situation is different,' Titty protested to Josh's shrugged shoulders, 'or if the patient is unresponsive.'

'Rubbish. My sisters were in Essex training as beauticians. They drove hundreds of miles to do her hair and make-up because they it made her feel feminine, womanly, in the midst of such undignified treatment. *Steph's Grooming Parlour*, we called it. They didn't stop coming to the hospital when mum's hair fell out or her cancer spread and she didn't care whether it was lipgloss or lipstick.'

'*Steph's Grooming Parlour?*'

'Yeah,' Josh smiled.

Titty glimpsed the name tattooed onto the underside of his wrist – Steph – and was ashamed that she had thought it was a woman he'd bedded.

'My parents are too busy saving lives to visit,' she excused them, a reflex reaction, 'so it would be grossly unfair of me to complain.'

'People can make time if they care enough,' Josh said, with disarming bluntness.

Titty never criticised her family. Nor did she blaspheme. But his bluntness and the potent liquor lubricated the hinges on her floodgates until honesty poured out.

'My parents are bastards for abandoning Oliver,' she slammed the glass on the worktop. 'For considering him an embarrassment to the family and for wanting him dead and buried so they don't have to deal with any awkward questions.'

'Awkward questions?'

'Yes, about his surfing.'

'Not la-di-da enough?'

'Yep. They didn't want to admit that Oliver was a bit of a wild child.'

'It must have been awful to rock up at the ICU all alone when he first had the accident.'

'Awful is an understatement. Before the Cornish lifeguard specified the severity of Oliver's injuries, I could gauge it was serious. It felt like I'd been socker-punched in the gut. I got umpteen speeding tickets tearing across the country, London to Bristol, doing 100 m.p.h. on the M4 and 80 m.p.h. on the A-roads. I shouldn't have been driving in that state. But, come hell or high water, I had to reach him.'

'It's like a primitive, primal need.'

'Exactly.'

'Was Oliver alert when you got there?'

'No, he was taken for a head CT, MRI, a battery of tests. The damage was undeniable, but It didn't stop me ringing every neurologist in my address book for a second opinion.'

'So you didn't get a proper chance to say goodbye?'

'No, that's the cruellest part.'

'Maybe there's still a chance.'

'His odds diminish by the day.'

'Does he make any movement?'

'Some. His eyes tend to be in a fixed position, but they occasionally track moving objects or move in an unsynchronised way. He has a sleep-wake cycle whereas other patients are in a state of chronic wakefulness and he can swallow or smile or grind his teeth but none of these things are a sign of consciousness.'

'Does he register your presence on the ward?'

'Neurologists aren't sure and Roderick thinks I'm crazy, but I believe he knows I'm there.'

We found love in a hopeless place, we found love in a hopeless place, we found love in a hopeless place…

'Wicked track,' Josh turned up Rihanna on the Bluetooth Wi-Fi wireless all-in-one music system.

Titty nodded.

'You know this song?' he stared, agog, as the doctor slung off her black patent courts and strutted onto the makeshift dancefloor in stockinged feet.

'No, I just feel like dancing,' she moved to the beat.

Adept at waltzes, foxtrots and quicksteps from a lifetime of cotillions, debutante balls and formal dances, free-styling was a first for Titty since boarding school. Although fear of detention meant dormitory room curtains were closed, music low, lyrics muffled, when the girls jumped on the bunk beds playing air-guitar. Inhibitions diluted by alcohol, she discovered the joy of spontaneous movement.

'Professor Wedgewood-Beaverbrook would have a heart attack if he could see you now,' the footballer laughed.

Pulling the kirby grips out of her neat bun, Titty let his hands trace the contours of her hourglass curves and slide down to her hips as they undulated in sync. Voices of doubt were deafened by the booming base.

'God, this feels good,' she moaned with pleasure.

'I bet there aren't many consultants who can bump and grind.'

'Ha, well, I'm still just a registrar.'

'It's only a matter of time.'

'What's that supposed to mean?' Titty spun around to face the footballer whose retort had cut through her hallucinogenic trance.

'Don't be coy,' he teased, 'we both know you're riding on Wedgewood-Beaverbrook coattails. At least I paved my own way to success. I didn't rely on daddy exploiting contacts on the hospital's board of governors.'

Titty's fall to Earth was a crash landing and her tirade coincided with a lull in the music.

'Have you ever considered that I didn't want to be a cardiologist?' she lambasted.

'What, too much money, prestige, knowledge?' Josh mocked. 'I can almost hear the violins.'

'A privileged upbringing entails huge sacrifices.'

'Only one trip to Klosters a year?'

'If I rebel, I will be ostracised just like my brother. Surviving as a Wedgewood-Beaverbrook requires unwavering obedience. A willingness to surrender all your personal hopes and dreams. I'm not a natural scientist. It takes all my bloody time to pass these exams. I wanted to study literature. But I was scared of rejection so I conformed.'

Josh's smirk faded.

'I guess that makes me an inverted snob,' he admitted.

We found love in a hopeless place, we found love in a hopeless place, we found love in a hopeless place

Revitalised by the pulsating chorus, Titty danced off their serious interlude, aware his body gyrated behind hers. She should have been disturbed by the frisson of sexual energy. Lust. Intimacy. But his body was a magnet. She was too drunk to fight the attraction.

'You're beautiful,' Josh whispered, hands slipping beneath the skinny black patent belt of her navy pencil skirt.

Damn, Titty realised, Roderick had never touched her like this. She pulled Josh's t-shirt off. Legs wrapped around his torso, he carried her onto the leather ottoman. He unhooked her silk balcony bra and she crawled on top of him.

CHAPTER 21

In reality, Zoë was the patient recovering from invasive surgery, but Titty looked more cut up.

'Sorry if I offended you…' she began, presuming her last-minute text was the problem.

Titty gazed, vacantly, out the window. She felt as if *I'VE SHAGGED YOUR FIANCÉ* was tattooed across her forehead. She constantly checked to confirm visible traces – smudged lipstick, palm imprints – had been eradicated. If only the memories could be scrubbed off using soap and water.

'…but I know you'd have thwarted the procedure and raked over the risks. Scar tissue, ruptures, allergic reactions. And you'd have condemned Mr Shiraz to a death stare or worse.'

'Yes, he should be struck off.'

Titty despised cosmetic surgery and labelled its practitioners "exploitative money-mad butchers". The scourge of surgeons. Yet nips-and-tucks were pushed to the periphery by fitful flashbacks of her treachery. Sex with John was perfunctory, once-a-week or less, in the missionary position. The Earth had never moved. It was simply another obligation on their to-do list. But Josh's approach was vastly different. Clothes discarded, bodies melded in the throes of passion, his hand clamped over her mouth. Bottling the climax to make it more intense.

'And I'm sorry about the grapes,' Zoë added, preening her voluminous tresses blowdried at the clinic's salon after paying a nurse to push her wheelchair down to the beauty bar.

With the ban on make-up lifted, she had recommitted to her beauty regime. Had her brows re-tattooed, gel eyeliner, bronzer and lipgloss for a fuller pout and her Electric Emerald toes to match her tracksuit were currently tickled by spongey foam separators following a pedicure. She asked Charlotte to spray her in YSL's Opium, her signature scent. Like her, it was controversial (almost withdrawn because of the name) and contained notes of femininity – carnations, mandarin orange and jasmine – and exotic Bergamot and spice that combined to create an alluring, captivating and provocative scent.

Titty's get well soon gift was impossible to dislike. But the WAGs had axed grapes. Exotic berries packed with antioxidants were the latest superfood.

'Sophie reckons Goji berries have fat-busting powers,' she repeated the advice.

Charlotte stopped munching. Instead, she ransacked the Custard Creams in her Radley bucket bag. This hoard of calorific snacks alongside the obligatory bland starches were now needed to replicate a 6-month baby bump.

'They're surprisingly tasty,' the WAG offered a shrivelled red berry as a conciliatory token.

A responsible cardiologist, Titty recommended Goji berries to patients as a remedy for heart disease. But she affected ignorance. Guilt-stricken, it was easier to abuse the food pretext.

ZOSH GET ROMANTIC IN ROME!

'Who's Zosh?' Charlotte noticed the tower of trashy magazines articles documenting the photogenic couple's city break.

'Zoë and Josh. It's our portmanteau. You're a bonafide celebrity couple if the public assigns you a joined-up nickname. Look at Brangelina or Kimye or Speidi.'

Titty, revolted by their PDAs at the Sistine Chapel, hunted for a high-brow newspaper. An in-depth analysis of *Cloud Atlantic*'s bid to monopolise Chinese television dominated the front-page. Harriet Taylor was pictured meeting media bosses in Beijing just last week. So much for slowing down.

'I rang your landline last week and John mentioned you had an ultrasound?' she asked the mum-to-be.

'Yes.'

Another fake appointment carefully orchestrated to clash with his seminar in Cambridge.

'And you don't regret declining the amniocentesis?'

'No, it slightly heightens the risk of miscarriage, and we didn't feel compelled to find out if there were any abnormalities.'

As a control freak, Titty would have preferred to establish the facts so she could formulate a plan.

'Dr Cranford agreed,' Charlotte lied to strengthen her rationale.

'Dr Kathryn Cranford?'

'Yes, my obstetrician.'

'I know her. Kathryn mentored me during a rotation in Obs & Gynae.'

Oh, Christ, Charlotte cursed, praying patient confidentiality was alive and well.

'Kathryn dislikes me less than most peers in her department. I might be able to get you upgraded to a better birthing suite.'

'Oh, no, don't bother.'

'Aargh!' Zoë cried, inadvertently saving Charlotte from creating a list of excuses.

'What's wrong?' Titty jumped into doctor mode.

'The pressure.'

Titty dexterously increased the morphine and repositioned her pillows to ease pressure on the wounds. Quick-thinking and kind-hearted, the action made Zoë reconsider her plan to bestow the bridesmaid honour upon Sophie who was badgering her for an answer.

'Mr Shiraz is a genius,' the fashionista undid her Juicy Couture jade green velour hoodie with her name emblazoned in Swarovski crystals on the pockets to examine his handiwork.

'If you say so.'

'It's fact, not opinion.'

Although, two days post-surgery, it was a mess. Tubes, drains, bandages. The cocksure cosmetic wizard promised her that resembling the victim of a machete attack was transitory.

'Confession alert,' she continued, finally putting away her puppies.

'You regret not going for an E-cup?' Titty hazarded a guess.

'Maybe next time,' Zoë said, envious of Charlotte's plentiful mounds in the V-neck of her wrap-dress that knotted elegantly at the empire line.

'You're eloping to Antigua with the dishy surgeon?' Charlotte said, fangs sunken into a fleshy doughnut after a dash to the patisserie on the ground floor.

Like a vampire, a dollop of raspberry jam spilled onto her frock with the consistency of congealed blood.

'You've abandoned your *Ok!* subscription?' Titty ventured.

'No, cold.'

'You realise there's more to life than Louboutins?'

'Warmer... I've fallen in love with Josh.'

Shock snapping her spinal cord, Titty was paralysed. Her betrayal appeared less heinous when Zoë's engagement was a sham. A glamorous pick-pocketing.

'What happened to footloose and fancy-free?' she stammered.

'Life is best shared.'

'Or monogamy was a myth?'

'I'm willing to admit I was wrong.'

'Or a relationship was a glorified prison cell?'

'Love is liberating.'

Before succumbing to anaesthesia, Zoë had an epiphany. If she died during this operation, her epilogue would be defined by snares and stacks of debt, a depressing legacy. She remained a material girl. But she made a pact to stop fighting her deeper feelings and commit to her fiancé.

'Wonderful news,' Charlotte clapped her hands. 'I knew Cupid would work his magic on you. Love conquers even the worst cynics.'

Deafened by their exultation, Titty fought images of her legs flattening the arch of his back so he could fill every part. A rare occurrence, she was grateful for Zoë's self-obsession. It might be her only lifebelt in this choppy sea of deceit.

'Oh, I meant to mention, the implants are a surprise for Josh,' Zoë explained, 'so can you two keep a secret?'

For different reasons, but with the same result, Charlotte and Titty were able to nod with steely conviction.

CHAPTER 22

'Strengthening your abdominal muscles may ease backache,' the midwife began, to Charlotte's horror as a phantom pregnancy required a slack belly. 'A common complaint during the second trimester.'

Charlotte mimicked the agreement of real mums-to-be performing these antenatal exercises.

'Well done,' John enthused, sweeping back her curls over the shoulders of her waterfall cardigan.

Urged to attend weekly classes, the teacher had pretended all programmes in the local area disallowed plus-ones. Horatia, however, e-mailed him details of this father-friendly evening session. Now, on all fours, Charlotte gritted her stomach a total of 10 times. It squeezed the gooey contents – toffees, cookies, nougat – into a nauseous clump in her gullet. Instant karma. Pelvic tilts followed. Flattening her back against the studio wall, she clenched her tummy button and held for four seconds, exercising the elasticated waistband of her maternity leggings.

'Six more repetitions,' John counted.

'Ooh,' she said, 'goodie.'

Like an exam adjudicator, her fiancé took his supervisory role seriously. Probably to compensate for missing the milestone during Chloe's development. Women gazed enviously at Charlotte. Their juvenile partners were a useless bunch. Here to snigger at graphic posters of the female reproductive organs or get stoned on the gas-and-air units. In many ways, they had her sympathies, but she would have swapped places with the fertile mums-to-be in a heartbeat.

'Pelvic floor exercises,' the midwife introduced, 'strengthen the area strained by pregnancy and childbirth. They help avoid the leakage of urine when you cough, sneeze or excrete.'

Each couple received a model of the stretchy muscles strung like a hammock from the pubic bone to the backbone.

'When are you due?' the neighbouring woman asked, features tense as she prevented an imaginary bowel movement.

'Three months.'

'Your first?'

'Yep.'

'It's my third.'

'Congratulations,' Charlotte said, exaggerated effusion to disguise her resentment.

'Any names yet?'

'We like Christopher,' John replied. 'Something nice and traditional.'

The hippie couple, Laurel and Leo, in paisley-print kimonos and bell bottom jeans revealed they had chosen Aquamarine (welcomed to the world in water), Nightingale (his first cry mimicked the songbird) and Fjord (conceived while protesting against nuclear power at an environmental summit in Norway).

'Where have you decided to give birth?' her tactile husband offered to give Charlotte a foot massage using his bum bag of essential oils.

John had outlined their triumvirate of choices – home, birth centre or hospital – and was strongly in favour of the latter while she was evasive.

'Probably at *Liverpool General*'s maternity wing,' he said, politely accepting a tape of whale music from Leo. 'I read it's the biggest in Europe and their safety record is impeccable.'

'I had our first two in a field,' Laurel elucidated, adjusting the Pocahontas headband in her raven mane. 'Leo gently guided them out of my womb. It was lovely to be in the bosom of nature. This baby boy's breech so I've been advised to have a caesarean, but we reckon he'll turn in his own time.'

'Isn't that a risky strategy?' John worried.

'The body knows best.'

While mastering the art of pretending to grip a tampon, Charlotte plotted to avoid more problematic discussion. It wasn't fair. Laurel had an army of kids; she didn't have a single foot soldier.

'I'm too tired to stay for the rest of the class,' she yawned.

John dutifully complied.

'See you next week,' the chubby, cheerful midwife waved, unaware Charlotte would rather walk on hot coals.

She remembered to do a pregnancy waddle towards the Volvo estate and simulated sleep all the way home.

•

Charlotte tipped the bottle of lavender bubble bath into the claw-foot tub. The water foamed. She inhaled the delicious aroma permeating the shoebox-sized room. Multiple layers – cardigan, vest, leggings, underwear – puddled at her feet. She sprinkled lavender petals onto the water and stepped over the side.

'Don't get too hot,' John knocked the door, interrupting her peace. 'Overheating is dangerous for the baby.'

'Yes, darling.'

Pre-empting his concerns about bubble bath links to thrush, she had already stuffed a towel under the door to contain the scent. John was definitely overcompensating for his absence the first time around. Now he watched her like a hawk, alert to her every whim, insisted on shielding her from all possible hardship.

'What do you fancy for dinner?' he called from their bedroom where he was changing into a casual shirt and chinos.

'Don't make a fuss.'

'Meat or fish?'

'I'll get something simple when I've finished.'

'Charlotte, you relax.'

I'm pregnant, not an invalid, she wanted to scream, but neither was true.

'Asparagus and prosciutto ham chicken breasts with Béarnaise butter,' he recalled the packaging on two protein-rich meals in the fridge, 'or hake fillets with slow roast tomatoes?'

'Chicken,' she complied, deciding the addition of butter made it sound fattier.

'Right, I'll put the oven on.'

Before heading downstairs, John turned the handle to try to grab a dishcloth drying in the airing cupboard.

'Charlotte,' he groaned, 'you don't need to be embarrassed.'

'I look like a beached whale.'

'Your pregnant body is beautiful.'

Firmly in the second trimester, Charlotte didn't care about the no-sex rule anymore. She refused to get naked in front of him. Without the push-up, padded bras that she hid in their underwear drawer, her B-cups and bump would be too conspicuously petite. But she had taken certain precautions and used a dark chalk to imitate the linea nigra, drawing a stripe from her belly button down the middle of her abdomen in case he caught a glimpse.

'Alright, I'll use a different cloth in the kitchen,' he averted an argument.

'Yep.'

As the only room in the cottage with a lock, the bathroom wallpapered in placid peonies was Charlotte's sanctuary. She relied on the fragrant bathwater to purify her terrible lie, remove the hardships and hassles of another day of deception, drown her problems for a few minutes.

She worked desperately hard not to overhear John's phonecall with Chloe. The poor child was sobbing from Horatia's lacerating criticism after losing the national under-11s grand chess finale in Newcastle. Little did she know that her place on the board was a pawn, movements secretly controlled by Horatia and Charlotte, two wicked queens.

Beep. Beep.

Charlotte wiped her wet fingers on a flowery flannel balanced on the taps and checked her mobile phone next to the soap dish.

Make Chloe enter Spelling Bee

She postponed a reply to Horatia and let the water imbue her with an illusion of weightless freedom. Unfortunately, dinner soon beckoned. She grasped her fluffy towel from the peg and dried off.

As she tied her dressing gown, John suddenly blindfolded his fiancée with a bandana fashioned from his paisley-print neck tie.

'Goodness gracious,' she exclaimed.

Leaving wet footprints on the deep-pile beige carpet, he directed her into the spare room.

'Ta-dah!' John released the knot.

Powder blue emulsion. Owl, fox, squirrel, hedgehog, raccoon and bird mobile and wall silhouettes. White furniture, polka-dot blue bedding, a woodland animal tufted wool rug. Dozens of fabric deer sown onto a satin lampshade beside the cot. A plush chestnut-coated rocking horse. Gobsmacked, Charlotte replayed the last few days. He declared their part-time study was off limits due to a burst pipe. It was obviously a ruse to do this nursery redecoration as he had concerns about pregnancy and paint fumes.

'I bought you a present,' he pointed to a photo frame on the chest of drawers.

Charlotte inspected its oval apertures for 3D casts – baby's hand, foot, hand – and tears plopped like torrential rain onto the sterling silver rim.

'We've got 30 days to exchange it,' John misinterpreted.

'No,' she said, 'it's wonderful.'

As he patted the food bump, Charlotte momentarily believed her own lie, that the bump was a baby who would blossom in this beautiful bedroom.

CHAPTER 23

'Atrial fibrillation,' Titty harangued, 'is when the heart beats abnormally fast.'

Meaning business in a cobalt suit, Ms Taylor obstinately refused to pause the letter to the President of the Peoples' Republic of China that she was composing on her iPad.

'It was a flare-up,' she asserted, stiffening the notched collar of her boxy blazer. 'Just a bit of breathlessness. A one-off. A flash-in-the-pan.'

'I'm afraid your description is woefully inaccurate,' Titty said. 'It's atrial fibrillation. Therefore, I would recommend an artificial pacemaker. The coronary angioplasty that I performed in February has been rendered insufficient because you have declined the thrombolysis medication, cardiac rehab and improvements to your diet and lifestyle.'

With a spasm of anger, Ms Taylor threw her iPad on the floor. She had been admitted overnight with acute shortness of breath. This episode triggered a repeat and she fumbled for the oxygen mask.

'A surgically-implanted pacemaker,' Dr Wedgewood-Beaverbrook swiftly recovered the tablet, 'is a small electrical device that should effectively regulate your heartbeat.'

'I'm poised to sign a $30 million dollar deal with the Chinese president that will revolutionise television in the Far East. I can't possibly take compassionate leave at this crucial moment.'

'Ms Taylor, inserting a pacemaker is a quick and safe operation.'

'Save the pep talk for a more gullible patient,' she interrupted. 'You don't care whether or not I consent. You simply want to avoid a death on your hands because it would stain your flawless record.'

Dr Wedgewood-Beaverbrook had met her match so she lowered her voice and skipped the pleasantries.

'Letting a patient with cardiovascular disease refuse consent to a life-saving operation is not desirable when you're trying to make consultant. So, if you won't do it for yourself, do me a favour. Bear in mind the procedure is performed under local anaesthetic which greatly reduces the recovery time.'

Realising her CEO duties would scarcely be impacted, Harriet's breathing stabilised.

'Do I have your consent?' Dr Wedgewood-Beaverbrook sought confirmation.

'Yes, alright.'

'As a precaution,' she recited the disclaimer, 'avoid strenuous activities for four to six weeks. You should also attend regular check-up appointments.'

Predictably, Ms Taylor shirked the advice.

'I'll schedule a theatre slot.'

'For when?'

'Probably next week given that you're classed an emergency patient.'

'Well,' Harriet tapped her tablet, 'I have an 0800 flight to NYC on Monday, I'm off to China for negotiations on Wednesday, but I should be in the Liverpool office on Thursday.'

'Thursday it is,' Titty said, retracting the pencil pleat curtain.

The sharp griffes of her engagement ring snagged its material and the memory of Roderick brought on guilty tears.

'I've got bigger affairs to arrange than telling tales to the Clinical Lead about how you damaged the curtain,' Mrs Taylor misunderstood her sadness.

'I don't give a damn about the curtain.'

'Consultancy exams troubling you?'

'No, it's a private matter.'

'Tell me.'

'I couldn't possibly…'

'The confidentiality clause can work both ways.'

Although a confession imperilled her consummate professionalism, Titty prayed that sharing the problem with a pragmatist, a woman with more grey matter than Josh's entire football team, might halve it.

'I slept with my best friend's fiancé,' she disclosed.

'Was it premeditated?'

'Gosh, no, we were drunk.'

'Do you love him?'

'Quite the opposite,' Titty defaulted to her prejudiced stance. 'We hate each other. He's an immoral, ill-educated footballer who contributes nothing to society. An oxygen thief.'

'So, it was a heat-of-the-moment mistake?'

'Yes. Nonetheless, Roderick and Zoë deserve to know we're rotten cheats.'

Paranoid Josh would carelessly spill the beans, Titty was a nervous-wreck. Eat, sleep, drink, all casualties of her crime. She had dropped a stone in two weeks and this square-necked work dress was baggy on her shrinking frame. But harbouring the secret felt worse than dealing with the explosive truth.

'Honesty is selfish,' Ms Taylor torpedoed her plan with bluntness learnt in heated boardroom debates. 'It's used to rid oneself of the crippling burden of a guilty secret.'

'No, it's the honourable thing to do.'

'Even if it destroys multiple lives?'

'Roderick and Zoë might understand…'

'Take off your rose-tinted glasses. Cheating is a breach of trust that neither man nor woman can forgive.'

The barbed comment pierced Titty's bubble of delusion.

'Roderick loathes disloyalty,' she admitted, 'and promiscuity contradicts my family's strict moral code. I would lose every shred of dignity.'

'Keep your mouth shut. The truth is like water. It only gets out if you create an opening.'

Glum, Titty nodded.

'Will your accomplice be discreet?' Ms Taylor identified a fatal flaw in their plan.

'So far, so good, but vulgar outbursts are Josh's speciality.'

'Then let's hope his memory is even poorer than his IQ.'

'Yes,' she crossed her fingers.

CHAPTER 24

Capitalising on a rare lull in trade, Zoë reread the solicitor's document. Love had dissolved her take-the-money-and-run plan so the pre-nup had diminished importance. But thousands per month in spousal support, a £500,000 cheat bonus if Josh's horse didn't stay in its stable, retaining all the jewellery and presents and "personal grooming payments" were a nice safety net.

Zoë Fraser, she signed on the dotted line without a second thought.

'Beside the chaise longue,' she instructed a Harvey Nichols delivery man.

Hitherto, splurging on pricy decorative objects for *Zoë's Zone* was a tad nerve-racking, but the document granted impunity. So what if Zoë maxed-out her credit cards, overdrafted, spent all her savings? Access to Josh's bank accounts was frozen until the "I dos". But he was infatuated with his future wife so clearing the debts posed no problem.

'Hello, gorgeous,' she petted the obscenely expensive formaldehyde sculpture.

Encased in a glass box, the razzle-dazzle cow with a glittery pink bowtie and 18-carat gold hoofs and horns was bound to polarise opinion, but she felt confident it would raise the boutique's profile and get it trending worldwide.

'Damn it,' the man groaned, noticing a traffic warden hovering around his van.

'Relax,' she said, stuffing a bundle of notes in his hand to pay the fine.

Zoë lapped up his profuse gratitude as she refreshed the autumnal window – hailed Cheshire's most creative display, a black opal komodo dragon swathed in wool and cashmere had a studded Valentino tote balanced on its forked tongue and rose from a blood red carpet of Louboutins to lust after a mannequin filled with gold feathers.

While she worked, her crimson Michael Kors tiered chiffon dress with Swarovski crystal poppies stopped passing traffic and her pumped-up cleavage in the neckline plunging to her navel made men stop and stare. Then Margot tottered past. Normally more conspicuous than a clown fish, Zoë scarcely recognised the OAP clad in a muted pointelle-knit cardigan, beige slacks and flats. Hells bells, she panicked, Margot was even pulling an old lady's shopping trolley.

'How's business?' the pensioner paused.

'Booming, thanks.'

'It must be due to your ban on grannies.'

A glass panel divided them. Yet it was penetrated by spikes of hostile air.

'You'd look a million dollars in our A/W Hervé Leger capsule collection,' Zoë appeased. 'Especially the metallic macramé line. Paul van Borgan will be putty in your hands.'

'Actually, Paul won't give a damn.'

'Oh?' she gnawed the end of her fishtail plait with concern.

'He saw the posts on Sophie's Facebook. Disgusted, he changed his status to single and made me the laughing stock of Wall Street.'

Zoë now realised the prank courtesy of Paul alias The Prat had sucked the joie de vivre out of Margot like a vacuum-pack bag until the customer was a withered shell of her former self.

'I'm so sorry,' she was racked with remorse.

'£1,480?' Margot peered at the price tag of the Valentino tote. 'I hoped to cheer myself up with a new bit of arm candy, but it was a pipe dream, clearly.'

'50% off. Today only. Mates rates.'

'Well, I do love the rock-chick studs,' she ventured a half-smile.

Like a burst of ambi-pur, the air felt fresher, and the social butterflies chatted merrily.

'I've found a wedding venue,' Zoë said, handing Margot the luxury brochure as they relocated to the chaise longue. 'Farthing Barn in Gloucestershire. *Ok!* has already bid for the photo rights.'

'Ching ching,' she joshed.

'And the hen party's in Vegas.'

'In my heyday,' Margot reminisced, 'I was the belle of the Bright Light city. The go-to gal of the Rat Pack. Frank Sinatra said I was the one who got away.'

'Ha, well, I'd love your opinion on the wedding cake.'

'Happy to help.'

Suddenly, Sophie's fire engine red Lamborghini sped to a stop outside the boutique where the oak trees that punctuated pavements and parking bays were a seasonal barometer, their leaves browning in the pale September sunshine as if they'd undergone expensive lowlights at a hairdressing salon.

'This is *Zoë's Zone*,' the WAG dismissed, flicking Margot away with a cheetah-print talon whose crassness matched her denim jumpsuit, 'not *Help the Aged*.'

Once again, its owner imitated the callous behaviour, ignoring pinpricks of regret as she converted from Jekyll to Hyde.

'OMG,' Sophie gasped, 'was the dinosaur trying to steal that bag?'

'Yeah,' Zoë swiped the tote from under Margot's nose with a clatter of cocktail rings, 'I caught her with grubby mitts all over it.'

'Gross. I warned you that allowing old people on the premises is career suicide. She must be going senile to think Valentino was made for wrinklies.'

'Exactly, what a nutter, ride away on your mobility scooter before we call the police.'

The duo cackled as Margot, shakily, pushed her trolley to the supermarket.

'Christ, I hope you haven't invited her to the wedding?' Sophie glimpsed the barn brochure.

'Don't talk trash.'

'Phew.'

A while ago, however, Zoë had considered Margot as ideal material for a wedding planner – a fellow pupil of the more is more school of thought – and potentially the woman to walk her up the aisle. Now the bouncers would be fired if they let her in.

'Sophie,' she began, finally resolving a dilemma, 'would you be my maid-of-honour?'

'On one condition.'

'Anything for you, babe.'

'Return that pimped-up cow to its field. Pronto. It's a monstrosity.'

CHAPTER 25

Like an excitable puppy, Chloe bounded home from school and into the kitchen to give her stepmother a hug.

'Ugh, you're soaking,' Charlotte complained, noticing her uniform dyed a darker shade of blue by the recent downpour.

Arms strained from struggling to meet around her stepmum's thick girth, the child slung her rucksack over a ladder-back kitchen chair.

'I didn't want to wait for a bus,' she rested her ear against Charlotte's tummy for rumblings of baby movement.

'Silly girl, I'll have to get you some dry clothes,' Charlotte pushed her off.

Tender embraces with Chloe intensified the guilt of being morally bankrupt so Charlotte solved the problem with icy conduct – her inspiration was Horatia, the original Cruella de Ville – but acting aloof wasn't nice or natural and she was knackered from fighting her maternal instincts.

'Put these on,' Charlotte said, letting her borrow a chunky cardigan, plaid shirt and joggers.

'Can't I wear one of your pretty dresses?' the 9-year-old asked.

'No, you'll catch a chill.'

'Technically, you can't a chill because it's not contagious. Unlike a common cold, which is an infectious viral disease of the upper respiratory tract, a chill is the product of exposure to cold temperatures or a side-effect of some autoimmune and inflammatory disorders.'

'Don't be a smart Alec,' she snapped, 'I said no.'

Charlotte speared a pickled onion from the Mason jars on the windowsill to keep up her pretend craving for spicy foods.

'How was school?' she nibbled at the rancid vinegar ball on her fork.

'Trigonometry's for geeks,' the girl sighed. 'I hate it. It's so boring.'

Charlotte's ears pricked up. Horatia had issued a mandate to awaken her daughter's interest in maths ahead of a residential Algebraic geometry course during October half-term. She hoped it was dormant as opposed to dead.

'Angles, cosines, tangents,' she listed, 'are building blocks for lots of cool jobs.'

Chloe rolled her eyes.

'Architecture, engineering, construction...'

'I'd rather be a baker.'

'A baker?'

'Yes,' Chloe declared, wincing as Charlotte combed her frizzy wet hair as if her scalp had no nerve endings.

'What happened to zoology?'

'Um, maybe I could bake cakes for the staff and animals at Chester Zoo.'

'A tiger might prefer antelope carcass to carrot cake.'

'Then I'd make a cake out of raw meat.'

Sprinkling edible glitter over twelve cooled cupcakes, Charlotte put off the fight. Her maternity leave now equalled daily baking bonanzas, both a distraction technique and a chance to bloat her BMI. Crockery was piled in the Belfast sink although most bowls were licked clean. Flour smattered the orange-and-cream ceramic tiled splashback. Like a corrupted crime scene, the evidence would be destroyed before John returned from work to concoct a healthy evening meal.

'Ooh, yummy,' Chloe stretched for a cake.

'No,' she reprimanded, 'English homework first.'

'But I'm hungry.'

'You'll get a bite for every right answer.'

Competing in Roe House's spelling bee was an arduous task that required months of painstaking practise.

'Fine,' she sulked.

Charlotte wiped excess buttercream off her hands, smearing her Cath Kidston floral apron, and unearthed the textbook from the cluttered wooden worktop.

'Lackadaisical?' she asked.

'L-a-c-k-a-d-a-i-s-i-c-a-l. Definition: without interest or energy; i.e. listless and lethargic. Example: a lackadaisical attempt.'

Correct, Chloe gouged a lump out of the sponge.

'Quixotic?'

'Q-u-i...'

Chloe's attention roved to the cottage garden whose foliage was enlivened by rainfall. Her bug shelter buried in the rhododendron bushes handmade from logs, bark and pine cones swarmed with insects. The bricks where she'd bored 18 cavities for bees was buzzing – furry bees laid their eggs before plugging the hole with vegetation until their offspring was ready to emerge the following spring. Red Admiral butterflies fluttered to the fermented fruit on a glass-blown stand. A murmuration of starling landed on the feeding table to feast on sunflower seeds that Charlotte had arranged while salvaging blackberries and raspberries for a pie from overhanging brambles.

'I wonder,' she chewed a HB pencil in contemplation upon spotting the latest ultrasound scan pinned to the fridge next to a *Don't Forget To Do Your Pelvic Floor Exercises* on a post-it that John had written, 'if the baby will have blonde hair or brown?'

'Oh, um, no idea.'

'Dark eyes like dad or hazel like you?'

'Chloe,' she snapped, 'you have a word to spell.'

The little girl's eyes stung with humiliated tears.

'Q-u-i-x-o-t-i-c,' Chloe hiccupped. 'Definition: impractical and idealistic from Don Quixote, hero of the 17th-century Miguel de Cervantes Saavedra novel. Example: take your head out of the clouds, stop being so quixotic.'

'Correct.'

'Have you decided on a date for the baby shower?' Chloe persisted.

'Oh, no, not yet.'

'Well, mummy says I have lacrosse trials in October, Saturdays from 9 a.m. to 12 p.m., but the afternoons are free.'

Chloe investigated the new fruit and vegetable collage of *How Big Is My Baby?* that John had pinned to the cork board. It started microscopically. At 4 weeks, baby was the size of a poppy seed; 6 weeks, a lentil; 8 weeks, a kidney bean; 10 weeks, a kumquat; 12 weeks, a lime; 14 weeks, a lemon; 16 weeks, an avocado; 18 weeks, a bell pepper; at 20 weeks, baby's legs uncurled so midwives compared it to a banana; 22 weeks, a squash; 24 weeks, a mango; 26 weeks, a cauliflower; 28 weeks, an aubergine; 30 weeks, a butternut squash; 32 weeks, a cabbage; 34 weeks, a pineapple; 36 weeks, a melon; 38 weeks, a marrow.

'So, my baby brother is roughly the size of a squash,' Chloe deduced.

'Mmm.'

Charlotte promptly scanned the next set of words.

'Diaphanous?'

'D-i-a-f-a-n-o-u-s.'

'No.'

'D-i-a-f-o-n-o-u-s.'

'No.'

Longing to devour a cupcake, Chloe myopically analysed the letters.

'A speller has only two and a half minutes,' Charlotte pointed at the wall clock.

'Shush, I'm trying to think.'

'Remember the phoneme of physics.'

'D-i-a-p-h-y-n-o-u-s?'

'No, it's d...'

'I don't care!' Chloe shouted, scribbling over the worksheet, a slow-burning candle whose wick had finally snapped.

'Calm down, let's take a break.'

'No, I hate spelling! I hate you! And I hate the baby for making you mean!'

Chloe kicked over wellington boots beside the back door and ran away from a woman who she now considered a wicked stepmother.

CHAPTER 26

Founded in 1683, Oxford's Ashmolean museum was the doyen of the art world, home to treasures that spanned civilisations and former students of the hallowed university.

Tonight's Auction of Promises raised funds to support the museum renovations. But it was merely a pretext. This not-so-charitable event excused profligate spending and flaunting triumphs achieved since graduation.

'Winner of the European Cup,' Roderick exhibited a gold medal from a polo competition in Perpignan that he kept in the sporran of his tartan kilt.

'Impressive,' Hugo Hark lauded the maverick rider, 'but a CBE trumps a polo medal on the poker table of achievements.'

'A knighthood?' Titty questioned.

'Yes, for exemplary services to the eradication of small pox in Africa.'

'Bravo, old chum,' Tobias St Windhurst, a top barrister, fawned over his regalia.

Each aristocratic male at Titty's table appeared like a toffy-nosed squire from an 18th-century oil painting. A mop of curly blonde hair, high cheekbones, rosy complexion, pursed lips, unblemished skin. So pure and polished they were gender fluid.

'Well,' Roderick revealed, 'the Lord Chief Justice has supported my application to succeed Sir David Pritchard in the Queen's Bench Division.'

Tinged with resentment, Hugo conceded that he had the Royal Flush, aware a knighthood was imminent if he was elected to the High Court.

'Mr Justice Rutherford,' Miranda Hark applauded, effortlessly elegant in a beaded taffeta ballgown, 'it certainly has a ring to it.'

Loyally, Titty participated. Her engagement ring glinted in the crystal chandelier. It inadvertently stole his thunder.

'Oh, bother,' Miranda, her ex-roommate at Oriel College glowered, 'your rock is twice the size of mine.'

Hugo's wife hailed from a family of merchant bankers and the economics graduate who now edited *The Financial Times* would undoubtedly be calculating its worth.

'Size doesn't matter,' her husband defended.

'That is an outright lie.'

'Ungrateful bitch.'

'Cheapskate.'

'Moreover,' Titty played her ace, 'I am poised to become *Liverpool General*'s youngest ever consultant. The appraisal panel presented unanimously positive feedback. A formal announcement is mere days away.'

'A decade since graduation,' Hugo acknowledged, 'and you're still the golden couple.'

Sir Pritchard, boasting more letters after his name than contained in the alphabet, was the university's vice-president a.k.a. tonight's auctioneer. He prompted guests to peruse their Brochure of Promises. A sedentary lifetime of study and 8oz steaks during hearty business lunches resulted in a paunch that jostled above his cummerbund. His graying hair was teased into a side-parting.

'Lot number one,' he launched a bidding war. 'Seven-night stay at Hampton Hall, Buckinghamshire estate of Gordon Monroe, the Balliol College alum at Table 19, including private use of the Monroe family's helicopter and a week's membership of Stoke Park Golf Club that hosted last year's Ryder Cup.'

'£2,600!'

'£2,800!'

'£3,800!'

As the hammer banged, outbid Miranda Hark stared daggers at Table 24's winning couple.

'Lot number two donated by Elizabeth van Rotterdam, Trinity College alum at Table 16. A 1902 Tudor Rose necklace. Amethyst, pink tourmaline and violet sapphire gemstones. Shaped as a rose to commemorate England's heraldic floral emblem since the reign of Henry VII.'

'£30,000!'

'£35,000!' Roderick waved his paddle.

'£40,000!'

'£65,000!' his last bid silenced the opposition.

'Sold to Lord Rutherford.'

Weaving a path through the constellation of round tables draped in ivory cloths, an obsequious aide delivered the exquisite necklace.

'Consider it a reward,' Roderick presented it to his fiancée.

'Sorry?'

'For your dedication at the hospital.'

Once considering liquidation, Ms Taylor had propelled her to reinvest all her emotional capital in their relationship. Yet Titty's smile camouflaged a multitude of sins. Working late, overtime, laboratory research. All ploys to avoid close contact with him that intensified the guilt of her betrayal.

'Golly,' she felt Roderick brush aside a cascade of chestnut waves to secure its lobster clasp at her nape.

'Doubt thou the stars are fire,' he quoted Hamlet, a play his mother had performed at The Globe. 'Doubt that the sun doth move; Doubt truth to be a liar; But never doubt I love.'

The jewel adorned the bateau neck of her blush empire-waist gown whose sheer overlay of pink-and-lilac floral embellishments swept the marble floor as she escaped his gaze to marvel at the Rembrandts, Manets and Klimts backlit in the alcoves, pondering if the melancholy she perceived in Vermeer's Girl with a Pearl Earring mirrored her own.

•

A flurry of waiters pounced on the auction's intermission to serve hors d'oeuvres – terrine of garden beetroot with horseradish sorbet or fresh crab salad – followed by roasted pigeon, Aberdeen-Angus beef or braised Cornish turbot amid copious quantities of Château Margaux.

'I see you still won't eat anything with a flesh or a face,' Peter D. Thorn scorned her risotto aux legumes d'automne.

As the glutton smothered his steak in garlic butter, Titty smirked at the director of wealth management for *Barclays* in their San Francisco headquarters.

'When you slaughter the planet's livestock,' she retorted, 'vegetarianism will become a compulsion not a choice.'

'Over my dead body. We'll eat poor people instead. Orphans, runaways, ones who won't be missed.'

'Offy, ignore my husband,' Saffron Thorn slapped his thigh. 'Tennis-playing friends at the Hurlingham Club extol the virtues of a vegetarian diet though simply because it whittles down one's waistline, not for your pious reasons.'

Nonchalantly tweaking his velvet bow tie, Professor Wedgewood-Beaverbrook was dapper in an Oxford outfitters' black dinner suit with white waistcoat. He approached their table and smiled, warmly, at his surrogate son. Titty was superfluous.

'Good evening, sir,' Roderick greeted the pompous guest-of-honour with a firm handshake.

The men exchanged stories of drunken buffoonery in the elite Bullingdon Club with frequent *buller, buller, buller* rallying cries while their spouses made polite chitchat.

'Did you receive our RSVP?' Miranda asked, tucking expensive honey highlights behind her ears decorated with moonstone cabochon petals.

'Yes,' Titty confirmed.

'Hugo will shortly obtain his pilot's licence so I have chartered a private plane to the castle.'

Her enthusiasm did not affect Titty who miserably pushed courgette, peas and spinach particles around her Royal Doulton plate.

'You're the envy of all these female guests,' Miranda confided, to agreement from Saffron.

'Mimi,' she dissembled, 'my ring is not vastly superior to theirs.'

'No, it's not purely the diamond. It's Roderick. Oh, darling, you know every woman in this museum is hopelessly in love with him. We've been besotted since matriculation.'

Titty acted coy.

'Hugo can be frightfully uncouth,' Miranda frowned at her husband recalling a prank involving the dean of the Faculty of Law and a pig's liver, 'but Roderick is the perfect gentleman.'

'Yes, I'm terribly lucky,' she sipped the wine.

Ring. Ring.

'Excuse me,' Titty apologised, four bejewelled fingers extracted her mobile from a satin clutch bag as she slipped out of the museum into the chilly night air.

Persisting with a manic schedule, Harriet Taylor's pacemaker could not cope and a transplant became her last resort. But an inflated opinion of her heart's resilience made consent difficult and locating a compatible donor was a very protracted process. She wondered if this call was good or bad news.

'I can't stop thinking about you.'

Josh's lewd greeting made her skin crawl.

'Get off the line,' she demanded.

'I know you want me.'

'Idiot.'

'Wait... don't hang-up.'

'To allow you more time to take perverted pleasure in ruining my evening?'

'No, to ask if you'd ever appreciate some company when you're visiting Oliver.'

'Oh...' she was floored.

Nobody in the Ashmolean expressed a flicker of concern for Oliver. Out of sight, out of mind, the crème de la crème had consigned the rebel to the history books. Including Hugo, his dormitory buddy, the man who requested her brother's best man services at his wedding.

'No, I prefer to be alone.'

'That's fine.'

'Josh...' she embarked on an apology.

But the footballer had already clicked off. Titty gathered her composure in the street lined with Bentleys, Rolls Royces and

Aston Martins, the best in British engineering bought by an Oxford education.

Then she returned to sample a Merlot-poached pear.

'Work?' Roderick asked.

'Yep.'

'No rest for the wicked.'

How little did he know, Titty shivered, as her engagement ring suddenly felt unbearably tight.

CHAPTER 27

Nestled in the stunning Gloucestershire countryside, Farthing Barn would soon host the Rockingham nuptials. But not quite yet. Its current job was to stage a cross-county wedding fair. Tailors, couturiers, photographers, jewellers, florists and patisserie chefs exhibited their merchandise in the luxuriously renovated 200-year-old barn heaving with bridezillas.

'Bridalwear,' Zoë said, oozing excitement as she identified the paraphernalia that commandeered one corner.

The WAGs targeted *White Weddings*. Glitz galore, it was like a princess's dressing-up box, a treasure trove of bounteous folds of lace, tulle and silk on curved ivory rails. Both women were mesmerised by *The Fairytale* dress with a beaded lace bodice of pear, oval and marquis-cut stones; a rhinestone-encrusted waist ribbon and silk organza ruffle skirt with tulle layers twisting into a chapel-length train all paired with a virginal white veil attached to a diamanté tiara.

'The Fairytale,' Sophie read the tag, 'perfect for a winter wedding.'

'Oh, yes, it's fabulous,' the seamstress, Madam du Chantilly, preached to the converted.

Currently in a nectarine leather Gucci belted body-con dress, Zoë ducked into the changing cubicle. Although it was sales spiel, a blatant bid for commission, she believed the seamstress's words. That a wedding dress chose its wearer. How, like love, it was a spiritual union. Meant to be.

'Gorgeous,' Sophie said, photographing a portion of the bodice to tantalise sycophants on social media. 'But I must lend you my waist trainer. It'll give you that waspish look for the wedding.'

The extravagance sent Zoë digging deep into her wedding fund.

'Done,' she brandished Josh's credit card, 'next stop: wedding favours.'

They inhaled the heavenly scent of 6ft bouquets of chrysanthemums, roses, freesias, carnations and lilies at Smell & Smile floristry and circumvented a bolshie bride arguing with her mother-in-law over or at stall. A charming raconteur at A Snapshot in Time persuaded Zoë to organise a video montage of poignant moments in her engagement for the wedding reception. Then the WAGs decided to lavish Bollinger, Crème de la Mer, celebrity perfume and spa vouchers on guests.

'The Cake Castle,' Zoë eagerly approached a patisserie stand teeming with decadent cakes.

Sophie gave it the thumbs-down and cut a swathe through the crowds to reach *Cakes without Calories*.

'Ladies,' the chef handed them two forks. 'This carrot recipe cuts out sugar, white flour and butter in favour of dates, Borlotti beans puréed to the consistency of a soft creamy paste and bananas. Add in a dose of carrots, coconut and walnuts and you've got a delicious calorie-free cake.'

Tasting the vegetable medley, Zoë reserved judgment and moved onto the courgette cake getting its unique flavour from cinnamon, cardamom and cocoa powder.

'I'd prefer an all-fruit cake,' Sophie took charge.

'Certainly, ladies, feel free to try our Melon Mix.'

Once envisaging a four-tier iced cake, layers of Cognac-soaked fruit on pillars and vanilla buttercream piped roses, Zoë reluctantly placed an order for white chunks of melon cake to match the colour of her wedding.

'Be renewed, revitalised and rebalanced,' a beautician accosted Zoë with leaflets for pre-wedding treatments.

Framed by wooden beams, the WAGs gladly entered the beauty arena and dispensed of their Alexander McQueen shoppers to lie horizontally for a marine algae wrap, cocoa butter massage and a hydrating facial.

'Breaking news,' Sophie said, speech muffled by the restrictive mud mask not dissimilar from a cow pat, 'I'm divorcing Pete. Our relationship is done and dusted.'

Once coasting on a wave of tranquillity, Zoë's face cracked with appalled shock.

'What happened?'

'He shagged half of Chester.'

'That's awful.'

'Chillax. He's been unfaithful since our wedding day. Footballers are hardwired to cheat.'

Zoë grasped polygamy was rife amongst premier league stars – playing the field, excuse the pun, was a rite of passage – but the concept of Josh cheating was unconscionable.

'A mole at *The Sun* told me they've got pictures of Pete snogging an escort in a La Manga swimming pool.'

'During the lads' holiday last month?'

'Yes. Plenty of other conquests will sell their stories. Filing for divorce puts me in a position of power. I can dictate the media coverage of our split.'

'So,' Zoë was perplexed, mellow eucalyptus oils failing to calm her unease, 'why did you ever tolerate his behaviour?'

'I was besotted with the perks of being a footballer's wife – i.e. the instant fame and fortune and V.I.P. passes to A-list parties – but now I've got enough star status to be a success without his surname. Plus, our pre-nup entitles me to more money in the divorce settlement if I make it past ten years. Unlike you, I wasn't smart enough to add a cheating clause that promised financial compensation if he did the dirty.'

Sophie's lack of emotion was cutthroat. Both WAGs married for money. Only Zoë had introduced love into the fickle equation. Since the epiphany, she had viewed her relationship through a romantic lens, blind to Josh's roving eye and this was a horrible reality check.

'If Josh cheated,' she realised, 'I'd be devastated.'

'Then start hoarding Kleenexes.'

'No, he worships me.'

'Sorry, babe, but no WAG is exempt from being dumped when a younger, hotter, thinner bimbo comes on the block.'

Sophie treated the girls to a vampire facial. Harvesting growth factors from your own blood such as collagen that would normally be used to heal damaged tissue, this procedure professed to improve their effectiveness by reinjecting them into your face.

'You're definitely qualified?' Zoë grilled the young beautician as she prepped a syringe to extract 2 teaspoons of blood from her arm.

'Relax, babe,' Sophie said, rolling up the sleeve of her leopard sweater teamed with a black peplum skirt and peep-toe platforms, 'it's not rocket science.'

Using a centrifuge, the woman isolated platelet-rich plasma from the blood.

'This derma pen causes specific trauma of around 2.5mm into the skin,' she explained.

'Fuck,' Zoë cursed, demanding to be anaesthetised to the hilt before any painful procedure, 'I thought it was non-invasive.'

'You'll barely feel the acupuncture-style needles.'

'Expect lots of film crews outside the house during the divorce maelstrom,' Sophie warned her neighbour.

'Paparazzi?' Zoë awaited stimulation of her elastin and collagen production.

'No, I'm contracted to shoot *WAG on the Rebound*. The new 6-part ITV documentary will be a real money-spinner and it should drum up loads of fan support. They'll petition for me to front a longer-term reality series, talk show, autobiography, the works. Don't get bitter. Get revenge.'

CHAPTER 28

Rain, rain, come our way
Rain, rain, fall here today
Rain, rain, come our way
Rain, rain, don't delay

The dreaded day was upon her. Charlotte's desperation had plummeted to unprecedented depths. She'd have to reach upwards just to scrape rock bottom with her fingertips. This rain dance was a delirious last-ditch attempt to thwart her baby shower.

Lady Luck cocked a deaf ear. Dry, unseasonably mild, with a light breeze, Charlotte heard the BBC Radio 4 weather forecast streaming out the kitchen window to where she was scoffing pastries on the patio. A glorious autumnal day. Then the doorbell chimed. Guests started to arrive for the baby boy-themed quintessentially English garden tea party.

Blue pompoms dangled from crooked twigs; the trestle table clothed in Broderie anglaise was a whimsical display of finger sandwiches, tea and cakes; bootie balloons tied to fence posts mingled with towering spires of hollyhock; milk bottles were recycled as vases for bluebonnets, hydrangeas and sweet peas.

'Gosh, it's a beautiful day,' Titty said, embracing her friend in a cornflower blue silk empire-sash maternity dress with a touch of silver woven for added sparkle at the buffet table.

Just a few amorphous clouds hung in the sky and guests harnessed the warmth of these last few halcyon days, conscious next month could spill into a cold winter.

'More's the pity,' Charlotte mumbled, as she pegged a congratulations card from the Rutherfords to the strings of twine.

'And the garden looks spectacular.'

'Yes,' she agreed, solemn, sipping blueberry cordial with a stripy straw out of a mason jar.

Demonstrating her schadenfreude, John's ex-wife had created Charlotte's dream shower – an open-air celebration of new life within nature – aware it had mutated into a nightmare. Now she wore a sickly sweet butter-wouldn't-melt mask to charm guests and win over Charlotte's friends.

Normally a pitbull in heels, the financier had softened her stern style to blend into the baby shower and wore a Charlotte-style vintage 1950s teal floral dress with Bardot neckline, fitted bodice and flared skirt.

'Tea?' Horatia pushed a wheelbarrow of traditional, herbal and green varieties towards the girls.

'No,' Charlotte snapped, as if fearful it was laced with arsenic.

'More cordial?'

'No.'

'Glass of water?'

'No.'

'Pregnancy hormones kicking in?' Titty joked, opting for Earl Grey in a dainty bone china floral cup.

'Some people just get my goat,' Charlotte fought temptation to pour the scalding liquid over her tormentor.

'Party planner,' Titty was conned by the bitch, 'maître d' and tea lady. Horatia has turned over a new helpful leaf. I suppose babies can inspire change, stimulate a desire to right one's wrongs and make the world a better place for the future generation.'

'I wouldn't bank on it,' Charlotte groused.

In a blaze of matching denim shirts, dark-wash J Brand skinnies and Christian Louboutin pink patent leather cork platform wedge sandals, Zoë burst onto the scene with Sophie in hot pursuit who chose a cup of healthy herbal lemongrass. Bearing gifts, she inspected the arty-farty *Brooklands Primary School* teachers dipping onesies in a barrel of fabric dyes to create unique outfits for the newborn and understood her Versace baby bling was misjudged.

'The receipt's in the bag,' she proffered a blue crystal dummy ensconced in glittery tissue paper tagged with love from Aunty Zoë.

'It's very generous,' Charlotte was diplomatic.

'This is a god-send,' Sophie produced a gift-wrapped tub of shea butter. 'Massage liberally all over the body twice-a-day during and after pregnancy to prevent stretch marks.'

'Useful to know.'

'Babe, have you submitted a request for a push present,' the WAG asked Charlotte, 'or do you prefer surprises?'

'What's a push present?'

'It's a gift the father gives to the mother to mark the occasion of her giving birth to their child.'

'Oh.'

'Pete got me a marathon pamper package at a spa in Sweden. It was scheduled only a week after the birth so I left the twins with my in-laws. Naughty, I know, but very nice.'

Titty presented a Harrods hamper brimming with a hat and mittens set, knitted booties, a ceramic money bank and Steiff teddy.

Humbled by the godmothers' gestures, Charlotte sought comfort in food. She scooped a handful of mini quiches, Scotch eggs and sausage rolls onto her polka-dot plate. Alcohol was sorely missed.

'Have you been doing your pelvic floor exercises?' Sophie was forward.

'Um…yes.'

'Incontinence pads can destroy marriages,' she was deadly serious, 'not just designer clothes.'

'Most feminine hygiene ads claim to have manufactured a pad that is ultra-discreet,' Zoë added, 'but they're not invisible.'

'Yes, and none fit inside a thong.'

'Time to invest in Bridget Jones-style pants,' Titty was flippant.

'I'd rather die!' Zoë shrieked, melodramatically.

'Are you planning a natural birth?' Sophie persisted.

'Yep.'

'Well, if it's a water birth, get a full wax before you get in the tub because you don't want your pubic hair to flap like seaweed. But I would recommend a C-section. It's pain-free, the scar is really discreet, and you can get a tummy-tuck at the same time.'

Charlotte was keen to change the subject.

'Feeling cold?' she noticed the lower half of Zoë's face was swaddled in a Hermès scarf.

'Um, yeah, a bit.'

Titty leapt into doctor mode and the girls half-expected her to wield a stethoscope from her Burberry bowler bag with the brand's signature check.

'Let me take your temperature,' she placed a hand on Zoë's brow to inspect for pneumonia.

'No, it's really not necessary.'

'Chest pain when you breathe or cough?'

'No.'

'Phlegm?'

'No.'

'Nausea, vomiting, diarrhoea?'

'I'm not unwell,' Zoë intervened, lowering her scarf to the girls' horror.

'A trout pout?' Titty slammed the latest in a long line of cosmetic procedures.

'I prefer the term bee-stung.'

'Yes,' Sophie said, her own version slick with Lancôme's Diva Dewberry. 'Isn't it gorgeous? Now we're twins.'

'More like victims of a terrible medical experiment.'

'I knew you'd hate it,' Zoë moaned.

'Rightly so. The risks of lip fillers are dire. Paralysis, infection, allergic reactions. Some people end up like stroke victims through playing Russian Roulette with their bodies to conform to a ridiculous trend for a mouth like a suction pad.'

But Titty could no longer claim the moral high ground.

'Still, it's your body, your choice,' she allowed, forcing the red mist to evaporate.

Meanwhile, Charlotte gobbled her third pork pie, slathered mustard onto a ham and cheese sandwich and demolished six mini raspberry-and-white chocolate cheesecakes.

'I thought eating for two was a myth,' Zoë commented.

'Sorry to disappoint.'

'I'll lend you a copy of *Blitz the Baby Weight*,' Sophie offered. 'You'll get rid of the bulge in thirty days. Guaranteed.'

'I can't believe you're a mother,' Titty was shocked.

'Yep, to 2-year-old twins, Chardonnay and Champagne.'

'Calling your children after French plonk,' the doctor mocked. 'How classy.'

'You could have brought them,' Charlotte said, unaware they were simply fashion accessories.

'And spend the afternoon changing nappies, playing peek-a-boo and singing nursery rhymes? Entertaining rugrats is not my idea of fun. That's why I pay a live-in nanny.'

With a puff of self-righteousness, Sophie tottered off to take a phonecall from her divorce lawyer.

'Last night,' Zoë revealed, 'I pierced Josh's condom.'

Splashing her V-neck cable knit sweater with Earl Grey, Titty choked on the tea.

'Sophie says footballers are less likely to cheat if they've got kids. Her hubby, Pete, was 100% faithful for the first twelve months of parenthood. A record for him.'

'I thought you were opposed to kids?'

'Only before I met the right man to father them.'

'Does Josh want a family?' Charlotte asked.

'Yeah, but he'd prefer to wait until retirement, probably when he's over 35.'

'You can't trick him into becoming a father,' Titty was the voice of reason.

'I'm sure he'll forgive me when the baby comes.'

'You're insane,' she declared, more sensible than her beige leather loafers.

'Well, even if I don't fall pregnant before the wedding, our sex life is so voracious that an accident is inevitable.'

'So, the passionate phase of your relationship hasn't waned?' Charlotte asked, remembering to pat her bump like a ubiquitous mum-to-be.

'Nope, he's a beast in the bedroom. Although it's me who roars like a tiger. I don't know how you're managing to uphold John's chastity law, Charlotte. There must be cobwebs growing in your nether regions by now.'

Though uncomfortable with crudeness, even Titty cracked a smile and watched Earth-mother, Laurel, dance barefoot in the long grass wearing a homespun peasant blouse while her children somersaulted in t-shirts covered with peace symbols.

'Still no desire to make a mini-Roderick or a mini-Titty?' Zoë asked, captivated by Charlotte's nieces and nephews blowing bubbles.

'It's impossible to be a high-flier and do the school run,' Titty said.

'Roderick's words or yours?'

'Both. Mine and his. We're a team.'

'Me thinks the lady doth protest too much.'

Like a mermaid sunning herself on a rocky outcrop, the trio noticed Sophie was a lady of leisure on the padded deckchair, sipping a protein shake with a copy of *Ok!* that was essentially a scrapbook of the latest instalments in the lives of her fellow Z-listers.

'Ugh, Chloe's not coming, is she?' Charlotte released a sigh of pent-up frustration as time wore on.

'Maybe she mixed up the date,' Titty suggested.

'Unlikely given Chloe wrote it on the invitations.'

Charlotte's month of silent treatment by her stepdaughter was a double whammy of distress. One, Charlotte loathed upsetting an innocent child. Two, being in Chloe's bad books made Horatia's demands more difficult to enforce.

'Ladies,' Horatia tapped a flute. 'Games await. Let's start with Feed the Baby.'

Blindfolded guests spun 180^0 and, wobbling as if in a drunken stupor, attempted to place a milk bottle sticker on the mouth of a baby poster hooked over the branches of a pear tree whose fruit Charlotte had earlier harvested. Competitive Titty pinned the winner's rosette onto the lapel of her olive green herringbone blazer. Than guests sat on polka-dot picnic blankets in a circle for Pass the Dirty Diaper.

By the end of baby bingo, Charlotte's cheeks ached from fabricating a smile. She retreated to the scrumptious cakes. *It's a Boy!* flags poked into tiers of cupcakes smothered with blue frosting. Blueberries embedded in all-butter tartlets filled with thick crème. Marzipan babies topped a triple-layer Victoria sponge that Mrs Law had coated in cerulean icing.

Squidging the grass between her toes, Charlotte wandered down to the stream. One boy sailed a toy boat while his siblings examined a clump of tadpole. The fruitful bushes on the bank – blackcurrants, gooseberries and mulberries – were festooned with emotive messages that guests had doodled on gift tags.

May baby's life be full of joy
Motherhood was meant for you
Babies are a blessing

Finally, the drought subsided. But the water was Charlotte's tears. They hit the tags with loud, pained thuds and diluted the words into incoherent puddles. Their significance, though, was indelible.

CHAPTER 29

A donor heart required transplantation within hours of removal. Urgency was paramount. But cardiologists could not cut corners. Titty scrubbed her skin in the same methodical fashion as if she was due to perform a routine pacemaker.

'Hello, Harriet,' she emerged into the sterile area to join a throng of gowned doctors and nurses.

Ashen and afraid in the stark theatre lights, terror had stolen Ms Taylor's voice as Mr Gideon, the consultant, conferred with a perfusionist who would manage the cardiopulmonary bypass machine.

'This machine,' he explained, 'will keep your blood circulating during the transplant.'

Titty followed the patient's eyeline to the spectator gallery. It was crammed with junior medics who forgot patients were people. They stared like vultures gawking at roadkill.

'Dr Wedgewood-Beaverbrook,' she spoke up, 'remember to rebuff any calls from the press. They'd have a field day if my operation got leaked. Media moguls would dramatise this story and use it to undermine my ability to do my job.'

'Yes, I've briefed the nurses.'

'Dr Wedgewood-Beaverbrook, ensure my medical file is kept under lock-and-key. The press can be wily. Journalists posing as policeman is not inconceivable.'

'Noted.'

'And you have the name and number of my solicitor if something goes wrong. My will is very straightforward. Grant gets half of my assets. The rest is split between four charities.'

'Best not to be fatalistic.'

'Fatalistic or realistic?'

'Let's hope it's the former.'

'Anaesthetic, please,' Mr Gideon instructed.

Previously a benign presence on a stool behind the bed, the anaesthetist double-checked the dose.

'No,' Harriet said, suddenly, ripping the IV out of her hand. 'I can't do this. I refuse to be cut open for your entertainment.'

Silence descended upon the theatre as she decreed that consenting was tantamount to signing a death warrant.

'Ms Taylor,' he began, resorting to a cliché, 'it's normal to feel anxious.'

'I don't want this operation.'

'Try to calm down.'

'So you can have fun slicing open my chest?'

'No…'

Denial was vain. Surgeons had a morbid curiosity for guts and gore. Titty had rushed from the baby shower to assist. A heart transplant was a rarity. The elusive pinnacle of her profession.

'Women are warriors,' Dr Wedgewood-Beaverbrook paraphrased her guiding principle.

'Don't patronise me.'

'You're a female CEO. A "Forbes most powerful woman". Mentor to young girls across the globe.'

'Flattery won't work.'

'So, what's the plan?' she interrogated. 'Going to a different hospital, getting a second opinion, trying other medication? Every cardiothoracic surgeon in the country will agree that a transplant is your only chance.'

Emotional, Ms Taylor staggered off the table, blood dripping from her self-inflicted wound.

'Is giving up the right example to set?' Titty persisted with tough love. 'Doesn't it defeat your message that a woman can conquer any obstacle in her path? Including fear?'

'Maybe recognising your limits is equally important.'

'Rubbish. Imagine your heart is a business rival. Richard Branson of Virgin Media. The bane of your career that's intent on making trouble for you at every turn. Unless you conspire to get him sacked, Sir Richard will take your job, your company car, your pension and then your health.'

Like a dying flower, Harriet withered. Her thorns had broken off. Petals of defiance were shrivelled. Even in the aftermath of her heart attack, the patient had remained meticulously-presented. Now, groomed hair stuffed under a surgical cap, stripped of make-up and drowned by the hospital gown, she looked old and feeble.

'A heart transplant is high-risk,' Titty pinged her latex gloves in preparation. 'Doctors can't promise a successful outcome. But Mr Gideon and I pledge to use all the skills in our repertoire to reward your bravery.'

Sensing her fragility, Titty delicately applied a bandage to Ms Taylor's injury and spoke with rare sentimentality.

'Since February, your obstreperousness has made my job extra demanding,' she whispered. 'But the world needs strong characters like you. Vanguards. I want this operation to be a success. And not just because I'm too busy breaking my own glass ceiling to sort out the paperwork of losing a patient.'

Resigned to her fate, Ms Taylor lay down and mined her doctor's words for encouragement.

'Please,' she tugged on Titty's scrubs, moments before the general anaesthetic. 'Call my husband. I want Grant here.'

•

Four hours, thirty two minutes, not a second of boredom. Titty revered the epicentre of the circulatory system. The muscular organ, no bigger than a clenched fist, had phenomenal pumping power which she felt when transferring the organ. Presently, the entire surgical team held their breath as Mr Gideon connected the donor heart to the main arteries.

'Beat, beat,' she pleaded.

Nothing.

'Come on.'

Nothing.

Beep, beep, beep, the monitor registered Ms Taylor's new pulsating heart.

'Good job, everybody,' the consultant said, taking her off the bypass machine.

•

Harriet Taylor awoke in the ICU under sedation and attached to a ventilator.

'Welcome back,' Dr Wedgewood-Beaverbrook smiled. 'The operation went smoothly. You are the proud owner of a new fully-functioning heart.'

The patient sneaked a peek at the crimson zip-like scar along her sternum which Mr Gideon repaired using permanent metal wires and dissolvable stitches.

'Don't panic,' the doctor reassured, skin still damp from her shower after the intense theatre experience and fresh in a flattering wrap dress. 'It will fade.'

The scar proved to be the least of her concerns.

'Is my husband here?'

'Um, no, not exactly.'

'Stuck… in traffic?'

'Um, yep, probably.'

Fuzzy with fatigue, the truth dawned at a painstakingly slow pace. Titty deliberated her answer. Upsetting a patient recuperating from major surgery was unwise. But Grant the scumbag deserved to be vilified.

'Mr Taylor made the heinous decision to choose a tête-à-tête with the Education Secretary rather than supporting his sick wife. His telephone manner was awfully brusque. According to the nurse, he didn't even ask to be kept informed of your progress. Mr Taylor showed no interest other than to confirm the NHS was footing the bill for the operation.'

As evidence, Titty switched on the 16" TV secured by wall brackets in the hospital bay.

"Grant Taylor, the Defence Secretary," the newscaster reported, *"has been pictured today entering the Houses of Parliament with the Education Secretary. Mr Taylor, 59, is*

understood to be petitioning for schools to adopt a more militaristic approach to learning – teachers will be trained like drill soldiers and impose stricter discipline on students. Political commentators speculate it will be further explored in his manifesto should he run for Prime Minister in next year's general election."

'I'm so sorry,' Titty saw the sorrow on her face.

But a nurse arrived with the immunosuppressant medication and Ms Taylor's window of weakness was firmly shut.

'Don't worry,' she brushed off Dr Wedgewood-Beaverbrook's compassion with determined strokes.

'It's perfectly acceptable to feel hurt.'

'No… I'm fine.'

'Harriet...'

'Go on. Get back to work.'

CHAPTER 30

In wildly inappropriate stilettos, Zoë gingerly disembarked the helicopter, fought the blustery wind from its droning blades that mussed-up her coiffured tresses and trekked through coarse Highland heather to greet her hosts for the weekend.

'*Rutherford Castle* should be available for wedding hire,' she had been mesmerised by the bird's eye view of its beauty as their chopper scaled the mountainous landscape.

'Yeah, totally,' Josh agreed, offloading their monogrammed leather Louis Vuitton luggage onto two struggling porters.

'Deplorable idea,' Roderick dismissed, 'it's a family home. A paradigm of Norman architecture. Not a commercial outlet. It's precisely why the Rutherfords have declined countless six-figure bids to host major golf championships on the 18-hole course.'

Zoë's strong suit wasn't sentimentality.

'I know WAGs willing to pay big bucks if you rented it out as a wedding venue,' she insisted, embarrassing Roderick with the plunging cleavage of her cropped velour hoody.

Titty intervened before her fiancé extradited the ruffians. Physical differences were patent. The nouveau riche wore Juicy Couture; the aristocrats were country squires in earthy-hues of cashmere, leather and tweed.

'Smooth flight?' she asked, ushering the group through the portcullis.

'Like a baby's arse,' Josh said.

Zoë laughed, uproariously, oblivious to their charging sexual electricity whose cinders Titty stamped out with her knee-high horse-bit boots.

'The helicopter was so awesome that I want to take flying lessons,' she revealed an insatiable appetite for adventure.

Accepting a tot of sloe gin, Titty was preoccupied. A casual remark about a weekend in Aberdeenshire had whet Zoë's desire to live like kings and queens. Guilt made her powerless to deny the invitation but the next two days would be clogged with tension like sclerotic fat in the arteries of patients on the cardiac ward.

'Gunmetal is so trendy this season,' Zoë joked, accosting one suit of armour while Josh took a selfie with its duplicate.

Roderick confiscated their iPhones to a chorus of protests.

'Technology is a pollutant,' he declared.

'It scarcely matters,' Titty said, averting a fight, terrified Josh wold blurt out the truth in anger. 'The signal is weak, anyway, at this altitude.'

Gun-toting Professor Wedgewood-Beaverbrook in a gilet and classic corduroy breeks arrived from a spell of grouse-shooting with the Rutherford clan.

'Ready for a game?' he asked.

'Yes, certainly, papa.'

'About bloody time.'

Piling into the Land Rover, Roderick donned his short peak cap and drove them past his father teeing off at the eighteenth hole on the golf course to a patch of moor where grouse prospered. He served them a flask of soup on the bonnet.

'Woah,' Josh recoiled, as he distributed ear muffs and safety glasses. 'I thought we were clay pigeon shooting. Not real birds.'

'Don't be a wuss,' Zoë goaded.

'It's cold-blooded murder.'

Unruffled, Zoë spied a male with distinctive red wattle over the eyes and a lyre-shaped tail which fanned out as he flew through the cloudy sky.

'Black Grouse would make a fabulous feather boa,' she imagined it coiled around a cocktail dress.

'Actually,' Roderick disparaged, 'they're dinner for tonight. Mother does a splendid roast grouse dish.'

'Roderick, hurry up,' Professor Wedgewood-Beaverbrook called over, 'let's blast these buggers while we still have the chance.'

'Meaning?' Josh was suspicious.

'Grouse are an endangered species,' Titty admitted, shameful. 'Agricultural practices during the last forty years have substantially changed the habitat in which black grouse thrive. Farmers have re-seeded huge expanses of the land with rye grass so sheep can graze because lamb is a more widely popular meat and fetches a high price at market. However, reducing the tall vegetation equals reducing the grouses' primary food source and shelter.'

'Making them more vulnerable to predation from foxes and crows,' Roderick interrupted.

'And twats like you,' Josh said, skulking back to the jeep. 'I'm not killing endangered animals for fashion, food or sport.'

Titty was curious – the cavalier footballer shared her fondness for wildlife – but their similarities met an abrupt end because he stuck to his principles. To please her family, she extracted the cartridges from her tweed waistcoat and loaded the arms.

'Zoë?' Roderick proffered a shotgun costing more than the average house.

Constituting a tutorial, the novice watched Titty's parents enter a bunker to conceal their weapon as the birds had grown wary of guns. Grouse was a challenging bird to shoot due to its speed and agility. Professor Wedgewood-Beaverbrook committed to one member of the flying carpet of red fowl. Engaging the bird at sixty yards, he pulled the trigger. No remorse as it fell out of the sky.

'Keep still,' he advised, 'otherwise the birds will panic.'

Demonstrating the technique, Titty mounted her gun. A lifetime of shooting had perfected her skills. But it hadn't erased the guilt. She cowered in Josh's disapproving stare.

'Pathetic,' Roderick exclaimed, as her finger slipped and jeopardised a clean shot.

'Is it dead?' Zoë asked.

'No, probably maimed.'

'So you're going to let it suffer a slow death?' Josh chastised, jumping out of the jeep.

'I shot at long range,' Titty confirmed her mistake, 'it would be very difficult to find the bird in acres of woodland.'

Josh ignored the gunfire and stomped towards the trees on the fringes of the vast Caledonian pine forest.

'Oh, bother,' Professor Wedgewood-Beaverbrook sighed. 'As if we needed further proof that footballers were braindead. I don't want the hassle of calling Search and Rescue. Titty, you go after him.'

Harbouring a childish fear of the forest, she pleaded to be spared.

'This is your mess,' her fiancé was unremitting, 'don't expect us to clean it up.'

Trigger-happy, Zoë's enthusiasm for the Sport of Kings was not dented by the drama. She picked up her gun and fired a full round.

•

Deep in Scotland's primeval wilderness, Titty quickly lost track of the sports star and attempted to follow a faint outline of muddy Nike Air-Max footprints in the fading daylight.

'Josh!' she glimpsed a baseball cap in the canopy of scarlet, gold, ochre and russet foliage.

'Back off.'

'Slow down, please, it's dangerous to wander alone in these woods.'

The figure stopped.

'I knew you cared.'

Exhausted from navigating the rugged terrain, Josh's mischievous sneer was not welcome. She chucked a clump of soil at his pristine England football team sweatshirt and cuffed grey sweatpants customised with ROCKINGHAM branded on the rear. Josh waved his hands in mock surrender.

'Just a joke,' he said.

'Not a funny one.'

'Agreed.'

Boots buried in blaeberry shrubs carpeting the forest floor, Titty slumped against a birch tree.

'Any sign of the grouse?'

'Nope,' Josh huffed.

'Let's return to *Rutherford Castle*,' she said, darkness looming, consuming the light with increasingly big mouthfuls.

Like a broken compass, the doctor headed north, west, then north again.

'Damn,' she rustled fallen leaves with a frustrated kick. 'I've lost my bearings. I've hiked in these woods with Roderick numerous times.'

'Alone?'

'No, on walking tours led by a local guide.'

'You mean a pleb who's paid pittance to serve the aristocracy in the area?'

'Yes,' Titty matched his mordant wit, 'someone to feed to the red deer if we're attacked.'

Josh rummaged in his pockets.

'Shit, your fiancé stole my phone,' he groaned.

'Well, I have my mobile,' she divulged, extracting the touchscreen model from her waistcoat.

'Don't tell me there's no signal?'

'All the bars are empty.'

'Fan-fucking-tastic,' he clapped with loud, sarcastic thuds.

'Don't swear at me.'

'Oh, right, because Roderick speaks like he's swallowed a dictionary. What an idiot. Hundreds of thousands on private schooling and a law degree and he still turns out a twat.'

'At least he's not a football hooligan.'

'It didn't stop you shagging me.'

'Grow up.'

'Maybe Mr Justice Rutherford deserves to hear some home-truths about his oh-so-perfect fiancée.'

'Don't you dare.'

'Luckily for you,' Josh teased, 'the honourable QC can remain in blissful ignorance for a while longer because we're stuck in the middle of a fucking forest.'

Titty recognised the reprieve, but couldn't help feeling that she was living on borrowed time.

Hands on hips, they surveyed the scene, hunting for a point of reference. She identified a distant trickle. Josh reluctantly agreed that a river might suggest civilisation. They followed its meandering path and noticed the triangular dorsal fin of Atlantic salmon swimming upstream. Unwittingly, it was a walk further into the temperate rainforest ecosystem rich in ferns, mosses and lichens.

'This is your fault,' she grumbled, sliding on moist tree lungwort.

'I didn't mutilate a defenceless bird.'

'It was a mistake.'

'Yeah, because you meant to kill it.'

Titty unzipped her boot and rubbed her throbbing ankle as a red squirrel scampered up a tree.

'How can a vegetarian shoot grouse?' he interrogated.

'I don't eat it.'

'Hypocrite.'

'How can someone who orders pea object to slaughtering an animal?'

'Well, I've been put off, that's for sure.'

'Grouse shooting is a family tradition,' she defended the indefensible.

'Be brave and buck tradition. It's weird how someone so assertive in the workplace, who plans for every eventuality in her career, has such little control in her private life.'

'I'd rather shoot to kill than end up the runt of the Wedgewood-Beaverbrook litter.'

Josh's criticism took a malicious turn.

'How can you be a cardiologist if you haven't got a heart?' he snapped.

'The same way you can play football without a brain,' Titty retorted.

The sportsman sat on a craggy rock and raided his pockets for a snack. Empty, he was forced to inspect small clusters of fungus and picked a red-capped version with spores of white spots.

'No,' Titty cautioned, 'the fly agaric is poisonous. I won't be able to carry your corpse to the castle. Unless you're happy to be buried in the woods, don't eat it.'

'See,' he said, unable to resist a final poke of the grumpy bear, 'you do care.'

•

Four hours later, Zoë was the pauper at a royal banquet. Inferiority, though, had never been a complex of hers. She dined on succulent roast grouse with a glossy chestnut veneer steeped in redcurrant and bread sauce, fondant potatoes, game chips and wild mushrooms as if accustomed to the diet of nobility.

'Enjoying the feast of your labours?' Professor Wedgewood-Beaverbrook asked, needlessly.

'It's delicious,' she eschewed cutlery to gnaw a hefty portion of meat to resounding tut-tuts from elders criticising her undignified table manners.

A whoosh of cold air slammed the Garden Suite's 11th-century oak doors shut on a puny waiter and the sound was echoed by the barrel vaulted ceiling.

'Shouldn't we marshal a search party?' Zoë was reminded the ramblers had not returned.

'They've probably gone for dinner at The Fox and Hounds,' Roderick dismissed.

'Or be hopelessly lost.'

'If so,' Maud Wedgewood-Beaverbrook asserted, 'they must deal with the consequences of their dire orienteering skills.'

'But it's dark and miserable out there.'

'Getting cold is character-building.'

Though the Wedgewood-Beaverbrooks appeared caricatures of the elite, Zoë knew the ruthlessness was genuine. Titty's father had once bribed her to quell the flames of flirtation with Oliver in case he was attracted. Shameless, she accepted the £5,000 cheque and splashed it on a trip to Louboutin's atelier.

'Madam, more wine?' a sommelier, privately amused by the newcomer, replenished her glass of Châteauneuf du Pape from the Rutherfords' vineyard in the Rhône Valley.

'Yes, please.'

'That will be your fourth,' Maud Wedgewood-Beaverbrook disapproved.

'Is that all?'

'You've almost drunk our vineyard dry.'

'Then I'd better crack open your collection of spirits,' she eyed up the glass cabinet of exceedingly rare 30-year old Highland malt whiskies.

Squeezed into a lacy black Valentino catsuit, Zoë stuck out like a sore thumb opposite the women in tartan shawls, truffle-coloured cashmere turtlenecks and tailored wool trousers.

'Lady Rutherford,' she hated awkward silences, 'I hear you're an actress. Odd that I've never seen you on TV.'

'A thespian of my calibre doesn't accept bit-parts in EastEnders or Casualty, the kind of trash you watch.'

'I'm sure you've popped up in a few porn films,' Zoë caused trouble.

'Give thy thoughts no tongue,' she belittled the guest with a damning quote from the Bard.

'Mother is a graduate of RADA,' Roderick enlightened the fashionista, 'and was commended by the Queen for her archetypal performances as Lady Macbeth, Cleopatra and Desdemona.'

Within a chimney breast of Vert de Terre wall paint, orange flames licked logs from felled Caledonian pines in the open fireplace and bathed the dining hall in buttery light. Zoë's nosiness knew no bounds. Brazen, she gawked at the ornate grandfather clock; the mahogany bookcase replete with Professor Wedgewood-Beaverbrook's medical tomes; Mackintosh tapestries and exuberant 14ft-drop curtains, a melange of exotic animals and kingdoms; the coats of arms; the pianist tinkling the ivory keys of the grand piano.

'I understand you are engaged,' Maud Wedgewood-Beaverbrook addressed the WAG.

'Yeah, we're super excited,' she deliberately thrust her buxom décolletage in Professor Wedgewood-Beaverbrook's face as she leant to polish off the plate of mushrooms.

'A summer ceremony?'

'No, December.'

'The coldest, cruellest month,' Lady Rutherford poo-poohed. 'How absurd. We're all delighted Roderick and Titty had the intelligence to choose June.'

'How did you meet Josh?' Maud Wedgewood-Beaverbrook asked.

'In a nightclub.'

A taboo word in this social milieu, the titled woman spluttered on her ladylike sip of wine.

'When?'

'A few months ago.'

'Months?'

'Yes, ten to be precise.'

While Lord Rutherford stood to relight a candle in the copper candelabra, his wife's meagre interest dwindled to nothing.

'Gosh, it's late,' she exploited the chiming clock. 'We must retire to our bedrooms.'

'The night is young,' Zoë countered, still chowing down half a grouse, 'it's only eleven. Surely I'm not the only night owl.'

Lady Rutherford placed a theatrical embargo on further discussion.

'Good night, good night! Parting is such sweet sorrow, that I shall say good night till it be morrow.'

•

'We're walking round in circles,' Josh was adamant they had already passed this 40ft oak tree whose mightiness made them feel minute.

'You couldn't possibly distinguish one oak from another in the dark,' Titty contested.

'I recognised its weird ridges.'

'Impossible.'

'I did.'

'Liar.'

Using its *On* light like a technological torch, the battery on Titty's phone died from overuse. The forest suddenly became a black hole. Exasperated, Josh lashed out, knuckles connecting with the tree's coarse bark.

'Fighting inanimate objects,' she mimicked his mocking claps, 'a low point even for a thug like you.'

But both were too demoralised and drained to trade petty insults. Titty did not protest when he declared they would have to resume their plight at dawn. A sliver of moonlight led them to a depression in the ground lined with grasses, dwarf shrubs and vegetation.

'Ugh,' Josh leapt up, 'we've got company.'

'The human imagination can play terrible tricks on you in times of fear,' Titty had also done a stint on the psychology ward.

'I'm serious.'

Together, they watched a wild boar forage for grub, its snout sensing movement in the undergrowth.

'You've trespassed on its nest,' she explained, remembering the Highland guide's speech on these nocturnal creatures. 'But boar are vegetarian so don't get your Calvin Klein's in a twist.'

Josh relocated to a hollowed tree stump.

'Titty,' he beckoned, 'come closer. You're obviously freezing. I can hear your teeth chattering.'

She clung to independence even if a medical education had taught her that combining body heat, thermal conduction, was the key to preventing hypothermia.

'Worried you can't keep your hands off me?'

'Yes, I might be overwhelmed by an urge to strangle you.'

Comic relief undercut their tension. Titty narrowed the gap. He draped half his sweatshirt around her shoulders.

'You're bleeding,' she said, cleaning his grazed knuckles with a tissue.

'Luckily, I know a good doctor.'

Titty smirked.

'How's your ankle?'

'Sore.'

'Maybe this'll help,' Josh shared a pea recently discovered in his pocket.

Like a super injunction, Titty gagged internal voices saying this sweet had somehow triggered a shift in the foundations of their relationship. From foes to friends. But the voices reached fever pitch when his arm snaked around her waist.

'Stop it,' she smacked him.

'Just trying to keep warm.'

'Why did you come? Was the lure of a Scottish castle really too attractive? Or is this part of your elaborate plan to continually remind me of the biggest mistake of my life?'

Josh refused to answer and now the shift was strong enough to cause a minor earthquake.

'You're engaged,' she scorned, wriggling out of the clinch, silhouetted by moonlight.

'To a girl who fantasises about my credit cards more than me.'

'Zoë is a self-sufficient, independently wealthy woman…' Titty offered a loyal rehash of her friend's lie.

'Bullshit,' Josh snapped a twig.

An owl hooted in response.

'She's a golddigger. I like her. She's a laugh-a-minute. Feisty, fun and fearless. Better than most girls I've dated. But she's only with me because I'm loaded. *Sun on a Shoestring* doesn't exist. Don't attempt to deny it.'

'Fine,' Titty couldn't cobble a defense, 'but her attitude has changed. Zoë's fallen in love with you. She reckons you're soulmates.'

Dubious, Josh rubbed his cold hands and deflected attention with an invective remark.

'Roderick's not in love with you.'

'Shut up, you know nothing.'

'And you're not in love with him.'

'We've been together for 10 years.'

'Time is meaningless.'

'He supports me.'

'He smothers you.'

Titty's jaw locked with consternation. Pivoting sharply, she burrowed into a different section of soil. They spent the night in stone-cold silence.

CHAPTER 31

Charlotte hacked, snipped and tore the cheesecloth into ragged spiderwebs.

'So cool,' Chloe declared, hanging tatters from the banisters.

Riding a broomstick, she ran into the kitchen, refashioned for Halloween. Cauldrons overspilling with spiders and centipedes. A spooky paper chain of black skulls. Charlotte, in a grey wig and witch's hat, whisked meringues for ghostly treats. Spiders crawled over cupcakes on the worktops. Eerie eyeball cake pops were terrifying realistic. Clusters of white tapers dripping with blood red candle wax emitted a sinister glow across the dining table.

'Careful,' she warned, as her stepdaughter used a knife to carve ghoulish critters into pumpkins.

Admiring their creative genius, Charlotte sipped a goblet of slime-ade. Even John was involved. Stretching wispy cobwebs over dark bloom bouquets – crimson roses, dahlias, black peonies – flowers she had cultivated purely for this purpose. A black cat apron tied above the swell of her baby bump which Christopher hammered with his tiny toes. It epitomised domestic bliss.

Then Charlotte woke up.

'Oh, no,' she panted, fringe flattened against her forehead with sweat, the dream crumbling into a thousand worthless pieces.

This year, October 31st was nothing but a miserable memory. Shunned by Chloe, she had ignored trick or treaters, didn't bother with pumpkins, threw a cake in the bin. She felt uglier than the bile green Hubbard squashes masquerading as warty witches in the Halloween decorations box still hibernating in the attic.

'John,' she prodded.

'Ugh,' he rolled over, 'can't sleep?'

Worse-behaved than any fictitious witch, Charlotte ended this toil and trouble, conscious that her punishment might be burning at the stake.

'I'm not pregnant,' she began, bolt upright in bed as if already tied to the post. 'There is no baby.'

Woozy, John's reaction was delayed.

'Sorry?' he sat up, accidently dislodging the plate of crackers that Charlotte nibbled throughout the night as he switched on the bedside lamp. 'Say that again.'

'There's no baby.'

'I don't understand.'

'Our baby boy, Christopher, doesn't exist.'

Unfolding in slow motion, Charlotte witnessed his painful transition of emotions.

'You've had a miscarriage?' he despaired.

Charlotte watched his heart break. The truth of her scheming would set fire to the fragments. Agreement tumbled out.

'Yes, darling,' she took another dangerous detour down the slippery slope of deceit. 'I lost Christopher.'

CHAPTER 32

'Happy birthday,' Titty blustered into her brother's cubicle with a bunch of balloons.

Oliver had a dribble of saliva running down his chin in parallel to the feeding tube which she quickly wiped off so his dignity wasn't compromised.

'Thirty-three,' she joshed, 'you're an old-timer.'

On the way here, she'd passed a car crash victim stretchered into the ED. Restrained by a neck brace, his face was a mess of engorged features, a scab of burgundy blood crusted on the bridge of his nose, torso mottled with bruises, wrist skewed at an unearthly angle. But time had forgotten this ward. PVS patients lived an eternal present. Oliver was preserved as if cryogenic, unravaged by daily life. He didn't appear a day older than his accident.

'I got you something,' Titty trilled, producing a limited-edition boxed replica of HMS Illustrious out of her bowler bag.

She cocked her ear as if expecting a response.

'Oh, alright, I'll open it for you.'

Titty had spent a fortune on the 8000 tonne Royal Navy battleship because its daring endeavours embodied Oliver's approach to life. Since her commissioning, HMS Illustrious had circumnavigated the globe, trialled pioneering new radar technology in the Pacific Ocean and brought aid to the stricken islands of the Philippines after a typhoon. Also like her brother, Titty thought, HMS Illustrious was currently resting, out of service, docked.

'Do you like it?' she nattered, not at all encumbered by his vegetative state.

To act as sensory stimulation, Titty clasped his fingers around the model battleship. He grunted. Then he started screaming, howls like a newborn baby. It was a common involuntarily behaviour of PVS patients and probably unrelated to the external stimulus. But it terrorised Titty who felt she'd done something terrible to cause such apparent anguish.

'Everything okay?' the nurse paused at the door.

'I can take the swallowing, smiling, shedding tears,' she replied, hands over her ears so tight that the butterflies of her pearl studs jabbed her skin, 'but I hate him screaming.'

Titty endured the torture for five minutes before it became intolerable.

'Got to go,' she tied the balloons to his bed, 'but I'll return later with birthday cake.'

Evacuating the lift for a priority patient, Titty had to wait to greet her mother on the cardiothoracic ward. She adjusted her ID card pinching the piped waistband of her Roland Mouret pencil skirt teamed with a white shirt and patent black heels and took a call from John.

'Titty,' he began, ominously, conjuring flashbacks of the neurologist's pessimism when revealing the results of Oliver's initial MRI. 'It's bad news. Last night, Charlotte miscarried the baby.'

For the 30 second ride, Titty felt intense sympathy pains for her friend, shocked to the core by events. But she had to reinstate her composure as a meeting with her mother dawned. The lift doors opened. Maud stood, arms crossed, in a tweed suit trimmed by mink fur.

'You're late,' she tapped her Rotary watch.

'Sorry, mama.'

'Work on your time-keeping skills.'

'Yes, mama.'

'They're more woeful than your orienteering.'

Maud remained cantankerous after her daughter's irresponsibility in Scotland. Bedraggled, Josh and Titty had finally hobbled towards the castle the following day. The doctor's ankle had to be splinted and, chilled to the bone, she had caught a nasty cold and been masking the symptoms to avoid superiors imposing sick leave upon her.

'Seeing the pair of you like drowned rats was such an embarrassment,' she moaned. 'Although I imagine Mr Rockingham led you astray.'

'Yes, mama, it was all his fault.'

'I don't doubt it.'

Titty was shepherded to the on-call room. Sparsely-furnished, yet an oasis of calm, isolated from the frenetic ward. Her mother ordered a junior doctor languishing at the coffee machine to vacate immediately. Wan with exhaustion and surviving on coffee and convenience food, the thrill of surgery kept him motivated. But he hadn't bargained for this rude interruption and, not risking a ruck with Professor Wedgewood-Beaverbrook's wife, vanished in a cloud of angry smoke.

On duty, Titty was squeezing this wedding dress-fitting between a pacemaker and angioplasty. Each Wedgewood-Beaverbrook bride since 1880 had worn the regal garment. Stitched onto ivory satin, Chantilly lace appliqué Tudor roses ornamented the corset which blossomed into an opalescent mermaid skirt and came complete with ivory satin kitten heels.

'It ought to be tighter,' Maud cinched her waist with sharp tugs on 58 pearl buttons fastened by rouleau loops.

'No, mama,' she protested.

'Mother knows best.'

Fighting for air, Titty's ribcage was compressed, but fainting was preferable to her mother's wrath.

'You should lose a few pounds before the wedding.'

'Yes, mama,' she obeyed, though food had been scarce since the Josh debacle as nothing tasted nice on a palette of guilt.

'Chubbiness is not cute.'

'No, mama.'

Stifling a sneeze, Titty placed a traditional crystal comb in her chignon and detected the blue ribbon sewn into the silk petticoat.

'Ravishing,' Maud congratulated.

'Mmm…' her daughter hesitated, worrying that she felt better, more desirable, in scrubs.

Oxygen deprivation, perhaps, made Titty ask a mad question.

'Did Oliver like carrot cake?'

'Good gracious,' she recoiled, 'I can't remember.'

'Surely you must.'

'No, absolutely not.'

'But you must have realised it's his birthday?'

'I stopped celebrating that boy's birth a long time ago.'

Proving Titty was a puppet under her control, Maud yanked the dress strings to enforce silence.

'Much better,' she declared, unperturbed by Titty's fainting spell.

CHAPTER 33

Cowslip Hotel & Spa was a healthy eco-retreat that promised the ultimate meditation. So Zoë did not expect a booming 6.30 a.m. wake-up call that interrupted her restorative sleep. Or the harsh winter sunlight flooding her spacious suite as blinds at its floor-to-ceiling window panes were automatically retracted.

'Ms Fraser, good morning. We hope you slept well. Today's weather: a fine and dry day with plenty of sunshine, a light breeze and highs of 12^0C. Humidity: 69%. Visibility: Very Good. Wind Direction: ESE. Wind Speed: 17 m.p.h.. Please complete your ablutions in the en-suite wet room with the Spa's natural products free from parabens, petrochemicals, sulphates, artificial fragrances and colours. Breakfast will be delivered at 6.45 a.m..'

An attention-seeker, Zoë had fantasised about entering the *Celebrity Big Brother* house, but the reality of being surveilled, a disembodied voice dictating your movements, was very disconcerting. The hotel was a WAG hotspot, however, so she swallowed her doubts and plodded off to shower with a zesty grapefruit scrub. Although the exhibitionist still felt slightly uneasy that her cleaning ritual was being captured on CCTV.

'Ms Fraser, breakfast has arrived.'

In a towelling robe, Zoë was summoned to return to the all-white room that smelt like freshly laundered linen. It was dominated by a super king-size draped in crisp duvet covers crafted from 400 thread count Egyptian cotton in a percale weave. No artwork on the alabaster walls. White wood furniture with glass doors reflected the 360^0 panorama from this all-glass futuristic facility perched on a precipitous Cornish cliff.

Zoë found her invigorating protein-packed breakfast on the tripod dining table. A translucent vase of Eucalyptus and white cosmos was a simple centrepiece. Trying the poached eggs, she watched surfers tackling the crashing waves below and Dogs scampering after Frisbees and Sporadic locals trekking over sodden sand to inspect amoebic life forms in the rock pools.

'Ms Fraser, you are invited to attend yoga on the exercise lawn. Please wear the clothing provided. The session begins in fifteen minutes.'

Suddenly, the wardrobe door slid open. Zoë discovered a pink racer back tank top and black Capri pants with a stylised lotus flower on the waistband top. Both were exactly her size.

'Morning,' she said, joining her fit-as-a-fiddle friend on the lawn.

Sophie was flaunting a perfect headstand, platinum locks splayed, while mere mortals adopted the lotus.

Their Thai instructor abandoned her Zen, briefly, to scowl at the cameraman stationed on the black slate patio. Sophie's drama, *WAG on the Rebound*, had been a juggernaut success. Now a crew filmed her 24/7.

'3, 2, 1…' Phnom Pham initiated a calm transition into Bhujangasana.

'Isn't this coastline invigorating?' Sophie asked, stretching her vertebrae, bending backwards as if made of elastic.

'Yes,' Zoë lied, sniffing the briny sea air.

'I knew you'd love it. That's why I brought you here for a pre-wedding getaway. No bride wants to look haggard before her big day.'

For Zoë, a seaside escape evoked Sunseeker yachts leased to oligarchs. Residents of a millionaire's playground – Monaco, Bahamas, Mauritius – dreaming of their wealth on golden sandy beaches. Deep harbours lapped by azure waters. Not Cornwall in November. Though she had to admit the nearby tiny fishing village of Mousehole, one of Cornwall's most picturesque hamlets, exuded an olde worlde charm with its yellow-lichened houses curving around the inner edge of the harbour and narrow streets.

In and out, in and out, in and out… yoga breathing, a collective tidal swish mimicking the waves on the beaches below, ended the class.

The WAGs passed the hotel's state of-the-art holistic wellness gymnasium. It was like a flash-forward to the Year 3000. Woman drinking from wrist-worn water bottles worked out on app-controlled treadmills and cross trainers while others underwent 3D body scans to tailor fitness plans to their individual anatomical and metabolic make-up. Dressed like astronauts, some wore Equilibrium Suits that measured body fat, BMI, weight, temperature and lactic acid to adjust the imbalances accordingly. When a woman surpassed her aerobic limit, for instance, the suit's mask would produce more oxygen-rich air to disperse the lactic acid in her muscles.

Beyond the Hyperbolic Gravity Room, another corridor led to a sci-fi simulation suite, an immersive experience to trigger the fight-or-flight response. Guests were deceived into believing they were in real danger – attacked by armed militia, in blazing buildings or chased by zombies – which made them train harder.

Sophie and Zoë stripped to skimpy bikinis upon entering The Aqua Zone which exposed their matching liposuction scars. Silver power nap pods dangled above the green-tiled cuboid swimming pool. Two women groaned with pleasure on the hydromassage bench. The film crew kept the cameras rolling for the WAGs' plunge into an organic seaweed hot tub.

'Babe,' Sophie grinned, flicking through the spa brochure, 'let's try a snail facial.'

A revolutionary Japanese idea, clients reaped the benefits of escargot secretions teeming with antioxidants and proteins, and a spa technician brought a bag of the creatures to the girls.

'Sure,' Zoë grimaced, as two bulbous snails were placed on her face.

A moment later, Sophie guffawed, almost spilling her patented Green Goddess smoothie that was a sickly whirl of celery, broccoli and spinach.

'Dis-gust-ing,' she exclaimed. 'You're so gullible. It was a prank for the cameras.'

Fearful of jerking movements, Zoë hadn't realised her friend's face wasn't streaked with slime. That she was the butt of a horrible joke. Comedic fodder for fans.

'What a horrible trick,' she begged for the snails to harass someone else's eyebrow with their slobbery antennae.

The spa technician dutifully complied. Slopping watery seaweed over the snail trails, Zoë understood this was her first time of being on the receiving end of Sophie's cruel sense of humour. The hurt and humiliation must have mirrored how Margot felt. Still she sucked up to the bully.

'BTW,' Sophie said, 'I can't make the wedding. I'm booked to model Topshop's new swimwear range in the Caribbean. All the Victoria's Secret girls are going to be there. It might lead to more work in the States.'

'What?' Zoë was flabbergasted. 'You're my chief bridesmaid. My best friend has to be at my side for the happiest day of my life.'

'Oh, babe,' she showed no remorse, 'St Barts trumps an artificially-heated barn.'

Zoë was speechless. Her first experience of the Queen WAG's sting hurt like hell. She heard the cameraman zoom in to exaggerate her horror, a dramatic end to the episode, the clever cliffhanger sure to improve viewing figures for next week. Used and abused, she made a decision. Post-wedding, she would dethrone Sophie and become queen.

CHAPTER 34

Dr Bishop, the bereavement counsellor, occupied the chair. It was opposite a dull fabric sofa. A pine coffee table, the platform for a box of tissues and a plastic jug of water, linked the two. The room was furnished with the bare minimum so nothing detracted from the tragic tales of distraught parents.

'Stillbirth is very sad,' she agreed, head cocked in the universal show of sympathy. 'Particularly if there's no rhyme or reason.'

Soberly attired, Dr Bishop tucked her curtain of greying hair behind her ears. She was early forties, Charlotte guessed, but perhaps the grey was an occupational hazard. It was humanly impossible not to be affected by these real-life horror stories.

'I feel hollow, empty…' Charlotte burned with shame, thieving adjectives from a *Coping with Loss in Pregnancy* manual to boost the credibility of her lie.

'At 28 weeks,' John added, 'we hoped the baby had reached safe territory.'

Charlotte's eyes grew a watery film. It was lamentable this kind doctor wasted pity on her fictional loss. Or John had spent the past month in shellshocked grief. He remained her rock. Outwardly, strong and stoic, but she heard him blubbing in the shower or crying over the fake scans in the garden shed, anywhere he believed was out of earshot.

'Mourning is a slow process,' Dr Bishop advised. 'Don't rush your recovery. Take time to heal.'

'I'm so sorry,' she said, her stock phrase since that fateful night, like a record on repeat. 'I'm so sorry. I'm so sorry.'

'Charlotte keeps apologising,' John explained to the counsellor. 'She blames herself. I tell her it's madness, that she did nothing wrong, but she won't listen.'

'Assuming culpability is a very normal coping technique,' Dr Bishop reassured. 'It helps us to make sense of a senseless tragedy.'

'I'm so sorry,' Charlotte wrung her hands in despair. 'Please forgive me. I'm so sorry.'

'Tell us,' John pleaded, 'how we comfort Chloe. My nine-year-old daughter from a previous marriage is devastated.'

'Discussing the science of stillbirth, breaking it down into bitesize chunks, can make it seem less overwhelming. Don't be afraid to talk about the baby. Keep Christopher's memory alive by answering any questions Chloe might raise. Describe his hair colour, mouth shape, skin tone, if he had dimples or a kiss curl.'

'I didn't see him,' John said.

'Oh, right.'

'Charlotte wished to be alone.'

'Many women express the same preference.'

Sickened by her guile, the teacher rushed to the toilets. Tragedy had obviously befallen the woman in the adjacent cubicle. She released a guttural howl that rattled the divide.

Charlotte had naively believed the partial confession would clear up this cesspool of lies. But, instead, faking a miscarriage at this late stage of pregnancy entailed faking abdominal cramps, bleeding, lactating breasts. Even a blow-by-blow account of how the baby looked when she gave birth. And now John had coaxed her into attending a string of counselling appointments which she insisted were held at an out-of-town community centre to minimise the risk of exposure. Her only real symptom was a loss of appetite though caused by guilt not grief.

I'll keep your sordid secret, she read an incoming text from Horatia while sitting on the toilet lid, *but only if you break off all contact with Chloe.*

On tenterhooks, Charlotte had expected the miscarriage to prompt another egregious demand. But not one quite so awful. Chloe had hacked down her olive branches since the tragedy, too distraught to be comforted, but Charlotte was hopeful their tree of friendship with roots stretching back six years was sturdy enough to survive this storm.

The teacher splashed ice cold water on her face with a little extra in the nipple area of her cowl neck jumper to mimic milk production. Then she impetuously dropped her phone into the bowl of water as if it would somehow throw Horatia, more determined than a bloodhound, off the scent and did a walk of shame into the counselling room.

'You had an induced natural labour?' Dr Bishop addressed her.

'Correct,' she said, researching the protocol with secret trips to the library.

'I found the concept very traumatising,' John said, squeezing her hand, 'so Charlotte bravely gave birth alone.'

'I understand Christopher's funeral is still pending?' Dr Bishop confirmed.

'We can't face it yet.'

'In my experience, organising a memorial can be cathartic for parents. A chance to gain closure. Say goodbye.'

'Yes,' John got the gist.

'Remember,' Dr Bishop advised them, 'overcoming bereavement is a marathon not a sprint. There's no reason why you can't try again for a baby. This loss doesn't mean you won't find success in the future.'

Distracted by the waiting area, Charlotte glimpsed a huddle of nurses propping up the same bereaved mother on the brink of collapse. In comparison, she felt an impostor, a fraud, a drain on the hospital's resources. An insult to womankind.

'I'm so sorry,' she rambled, fidgeting with the embroidered dandelions on her knee-length skirt. 'Please forgive me. I'm so sorry.'

'Charlotte, the guilt will lessen with time. I wonder if group therapy sessions are worth considering. Bereavement can be a very lonely place. The vacuum is often filled with endless introspection, analysing your pregnancy, questioning if you made mistakes, things you should have done differently. Mixing with parents in a similar situation can end the isolation and offer a sense of perspective.'

'I'm so sorry. Please forgive me. I'm so sorry.'

'Charlotte, it's not your fault.'

'Yes, it is,' she said, a torrent of honesty overpowering the dam she'd erected so many months ago. 'I was never pregnant. It was make-believe. There's no baby. Christopher doesn't exist.'

Dr Bishop diagnosed post-traumatic stress disorder. Confusing events was a common symptom. Fearful of being sectioned under the mental health act, Charlotte fled the hospital. Its revolving doors hindered her escape. Panic stole her ability to determine which segment was vacant, to push or not to push, when to exit. Like her lie, there seemed no way out.

CHAPTER 35

Congratulations to the new consultant!
Roderick x

Suffocated by ambition, the promotion allowed Titty's lungs to inflate to full capacity and its alveoli to fill with pride. She was the youngest consultant in *Liverpool General*'s history. And one hundred Grand Prix red roses from Roderick proved she'd finally earned his respect.

'Nepotism versus natural talent,' Dr Richard Lam ridiculed the board's decision. 'The latter loses yet again. What a screwed-up world.'

'You're just a sore loser,' Titty rebuked.

'It wasn't a fair competition.'

'Denial is a poor coping tactic.'

News of the promotion had spread faster than wildfire. Equally destructive, the scorched staff hurled accusations of preferential treatment. It was true, of course, but it did not douse her euphoria.

Deliberately prominent atop the nurses' station, Titty put the long-stemmed velvety flowers in a vase of water near *thank you* notes from past patients which she'd never received. Residual doubts about her fiancé, like the silt that wouldn't budge at the bottom of a coffee cup, were magically wiped away by Roderick's romantic gesture.

Acquiring the consultancy post ratcheted up her respectability not just with him but the whole Wedgewood-Beaverbrook contingent. Titty's younger sisters in Cape Town had called to congratulate. Even a far-flung uncle, a brigadier on a military base in the Falklands, appeared on Skype to toast her triumph.

Walking on air, Titty glided to the modern outpatients' clinic. Cardiology had been a journey of epic discovery – pacemakers and defibrillators, arrhythmias, cardiac device implantations, transplants – and menial investigations like taking a patient's blood pressure or prescribing statins felt like a prostitution of her talents. But even consultants had to endure mundane days at work.

'Ms Taylor?' she used the tannoy.

'Hello, Dr Wedgewood-Beaverbrook.'

'No, I asked for Harriet Taylor.'

'Yes, that's me.'

The woman who responded was unrecognisable. Once harassed, she now appeared Youthful in casual clothes and her androgynous power suits were replaced by pastels and florals. The 80s perm was gone. Instead, a pixie cut showed off her features and she had a radiant complexion. As the only patient who hadn't simply represented a rung on the career ladder, Titty was thrilled by her joie de vivre. But medics always erred on the side of caution. She took Ms Taylor's blood pressure and launched a volley of questions.

'Any palpitations?'

'None.'

'Chest pain?'

'No.'

'Dizziness, light-headedness, fatigue?'

'Nope, I've got a new lease of life.'

Astonished by her clean bill of health, Dr Wedgewood-Beaverbrook queried the immunosuppressants.

'The only side-effects are better stamina, sleep and sex,' she was matter-of-fact. 'I've started playing badminton. Taken up tai-chi. And discovered kale is delicious in a soup. I've booked to hike the Inca trail, too. The Peruvian scenery looks amazing.'

Titty was dumbstruck. She had performed a heart transplant. Not a lobotomy.

'Surely you have career obligations?'

'I'm taking a six-month sabbatical.'

'Ah, is Mr Taylor keen to explore Latin America?'

'Not unless it enhances his CV.'

'So, you're travelling alone?'

'Yes, I bit the bullet. We're divorcing. Your rallying theatre speech had a profound impact. As CEO, I prided myself on being a lioness, not a lamb. Yet my marriage to Grant was cowardly. I settled for a straight-A student, the sensible option, the safe bet. Not a man who made my heart race, challenged my fears, swept me on a roller-coaster of emotions.'

Titty's ears pricked up. Dum, da, doh, she heard the erratic, pulsating beat of her spirited encounters with Josh. Even their arguments got her heart pumping more than sex with Roderick. Thud, thud, thud. Roderick's effect was slower, more predictable, consistent. Dull.

'Complacency is a terrible precedent to set,' Harriet went on.

'Roderick's my soulmate.'

'Soulmate or safety net?'

'Well, um...'

'Isn't it significant that you've talked to me more about Josh, the man you hate, than Roderick, the man you're due to marry?'

'No...'

Harriet Taylor stood to leave.

'Good luck,' she skipped out of the office. 'Congratulations on your promotion. You shall make a fine consultant.'

Titty was perplexed. Her promotion hasn't been formally announced. The appraisal panel informed her that a late addition – a stellar reference from an anonymous patient – had settled her job application along with a cash incentive from Professor Wedgewood-Beaverbrook. Its author was no longer a mystery.

CHAPTER 36

Las Vegas Strip was a neon-lit artificial canyon carved into the Mojave Desert that provided the sensory overload to thrill this hedonistic hen.

'Sin City!' Zoë screamed, as her cavalcade of flamingo pink limousines passed high-rise hotels, billion-dollar casinos and world-famous entertainers.

'What happens in Vegas,' Sophie excused flashing her silicone boobs to a Yorkshire stag party who were mooning transvestites on the sidewalk, 'stays in Vegas.'

'Let's eat, drink and shag what we want,' Tiffany joked.

'Cheers to that!' the hens clinked champagne flutes.

Stateside for just two days, enthusiasm toppled jet lag. The hens swarmed Cirque De Soleil, flirted with Elvis impersonators and dined at The Bellagio. Next, they hit Presley Bar for a night of debauchery. Multi-tiered dance floors, lacquer and leather walls inset with coloured liquors, DJs syncing electronic remixes. Synchronised strippers performed in a water tank suspended on steel rods from the ceiling.

'Golly gumdrops,' Titty gasped, horrified by the writhing mass of bodies in this drunken orgy.

Handcuffed to the hospital, it was an unprecedented holiday, and she regretted flying 10 hours for this bacchanalia.

'Mai Tais,' Zoë ordered, ogling the bodybuilder wearing just a bowtie and apron who moonlighted as a mixologist.

Bulging out of his black shirt, Aidan revealed he had come to America's playground to participate in a Mr Muscle competition to win a cheque for $1,000,000.

'Isn't Mr Muscle a household cleaner?' she joked, but the man who lived on steroids was bemused by the British brand.

'Tomorrow,' he said, making the girls salivate with a pectoral dance routine, 'I gotta lift a Cadillac with one finger.'

'No way.'

'Then I gotta tow a truck with just my teeth.'

Seeing Zoë was impressed, Aidan gave her a lascivious wink.

'I guess you're the bride-to-be?'

'Certainly am,' she pointed to her L-plates.

'Who's the lucky guy?'

'A football... I mean, a soccer player. He's flown a group of lads to Bangkok for his stag party.'

'What's a stag party?'

'I mean bachelor,' she corrected, using the American equivalent.

'Sounds cool.'

'Yeah, it's gonna be like The Hangover movie.'

'Enjoy your last few days of freedom,' he dropped phallic twizzlers in their cocktails along with a copy of his business card for Zoë.

'Woah, Aidan, I'm engaged.'

'What happens in Vegas...' the bartender teased. 'Hit me up if you wanna make it a night to remember.'

Mid-Atlantic, the WAGs had jettisoned velour tracksuits for all-American fancy dress. Zoë became a slutty sheriff with a toy pistol in her holster and stockings. Others were cheerleaders, Grease's Sandy, Baywatch babes. Her more modest friends weren't exempt. Charlotte got a 1950's Diner Girl costume with a checkered pink dress and white lacy apron. Titty was lumbered with a sexy slant on Maverick's pilot outfit from Top Gun. The playsuit's gold zip was dangerously low, (men had already tried to put dollar bills in her cleavage), and came with obligatory Ray-Ban aviators sporting the US flag.

Now they sashayed through a shimmering beaded curtain of light strobes into their VIP booth. Charlotte gawked at two topless girls hugging poles sprouting from a platform behind them.

'Don't be shy,' Tiffany, the reigning Miss England, grabbed her arm.

Titty was tempted to intervene, but wondered if letting loose helped the grieving process, and almost fell quiet.

'Feeling alright?' she pried, concerned by Charlotte's transformation into a party animal since landing at McCarran International Airport.

With pink lipgloss, stilettos and blonde wig, the dolled-up teacher was a clone of her new group of girlfriends and clearly intended to drown her sorrows in alcohol.

'You've never flown long-haul,' Titty lectured. 'There's no shame in having a lie-down. You've had a rough time lately.'

'Quit boring me to death,' Charlotte barked, like a stroppy American teenager. 'You're such a prude. I just wanna have fun.'

Tiffany waved her cheerleading pompoms and instructed the ingénue to hook one leg around the pole while she tantalised her audience by frisking the shiny silver stick before a crucifix manoeuvre.

'Did you hear Charlotte sleep-talking as we left Liverpool?' Zoë asked, batting her false lashes at a passing hottie obviously turned on by dominatrixes.

'No, Sophie declared I was a fuddy-duddy and relegated me to the back row of the plane.'

'Anyway,' Zoë glossed over Sophie's typically obnoxious behaviour, 'she was saying all kinds of strange things.'

'Such as?'

'The miscarriage was her fault… to tell John how sorry she felt… that she couldn't be a mum.'

'Involuntarily outbursts linked to feelings of guilt or shame are compatible with the PTSD diagnosis.'

'Yes, I suppose, but I still can't believe she came to Vegas.'

In agreement, they watched the primary school teacher straddle the pole with reckless abandon.

'Time for Truth or Dare,' Zoë blew her sheriff's whistle to prompt the hens to pluck a *have you ever?* card from their party games pack.

'Have you ever joined the mile-high club?' Sophie, the question master, asked the wife of a midfielder.

'Qantas,' Trixie giggled, tipping her Wild West cowgirl hat. 'London to Brisbane. First-class toilets.'

'Done something illegal?'

'Never,' Zoë said.

But, barraged by her fraud, Zoë's poker face disintegrated. They sensed a lie. She was dared to snog Aidan. Not such a bad punishment.

'What did you do?' the girls asked.

'I was arrested for public indecency,' she spun them a yarn. 'Sex in a supermarket car park.'

'Have you ever eaten a whole tub of ice-cream?' Sophie continued.

'Yes,' Charlotte laughed, the most likely candidate in this girl gang of lollipop heads. 'When Westlife disbanded.'

'Read a book over 100 pages?'

'Never,' Tiffany shook her pom-poms. 'Unless *Vogue* counts.'

'Had colonic irrigation?'

'No,' Kerry said.

But the WAGs knew she was an aficionado of extreme cleansing recommended by A-listers. Yelling I'm going commando, the liar was ordered to twerk in front of a bachelor party from Michigan.

'Have you ever done the dirty with a friend's boyfriend?' Sophie asked the doctor.

As if horizontal on a bed of hot coals, Titty felt her skin pimple while the girls anticipated her answer.

'Rubbish,' Zoë dismissed, necking a shot of neat vodka. 'She's nauseatingly loyal.'

Blindfolded hens were challenged to model pink playdough into male body parts winning points for realism. Zoë scooped the plastic trophy for her rendition of a 6-pack. Then she instigated twenty egotistical questions to test the hens' knowledge of the bride. Soul sisters, Sophie raced to a finish, implying it was ridiculously easy. The party dispersed to refresh their make-up or splash their cash on the slot machines and she reviewed each answer slip.

'But we're BFFs,' Zoë gasped, discovering the WAG's abysmal score.

Even basics like date of birth were disastrous and these twenty erroneous guesses were testament to Sophie's superficial friendship.

'I need air,' Zoë said, staggering out the emergency exit on the mezzanine into the nippy evening air.

Bright light city gonna set my soul,
Gonna set my soul on fire.
Got a whole lot of money that's ready to burn,
So get those stakes up higher

Choreographed to Viva Las Vegas, The Bellagio's legendary fountains mesmerised tourists pouring out of a raucous Elton John concert and others giddy from breaking the bank in Sin City with wins at blackjack, roulette, craps and baccarat. And Titty. The doctor leant over the lake where 1,214 pumps rocketed water hundreds of feet into the air to shimmy, twirl and spin.

'Cerise,' Zoë approached a true friend. 'You knew my favourite shade of pink.'

'Of course.'

'And you knew I failed my German GCSE for making fun of Herr Baumgartner's surname.'

'It's not a story that I'd forget in a hurry,' Titty disapproved with an affectionate smile.

Hand in hand, they marvelled at domes of interwoven jets backdropped by the 4-mile boulevard of excess.

'Only four weeks until the wedding,' Zoë counted.

'Getting cold feet?' she hoped.

'Just excited.'

'Oh.'

'I really love him, Titty, with all my heart.'

'Yes, I know.'

Zoë paused, a tragic confession on the tip of her tongue.

'But I don't think it's mutual. Ever since I had my breast augmentation, Josh's been distant. Maybe he's disappointed, thinks I was too cautious, that I should have gone for a bigger cup size.'

'Highly doubtful,' Titty interjected.

'Or maybe he's the one getting cold feet.'

'Possibly.'

'Or he's busy lining up a bimbo to replace me.'

'You're worried he's being unfaithful?' Titty was on red alert.

'Well, everyone warned me athletes were programmed to cheat.'

'Josh didn't act distant in Scotland. When we escaped from the Caledonian pine forest, he snogged you like a starving octopus. And Roderick had to use the ear muffs from grouse shooting to spare us from your screams in the neighbouring suite that night.'

'Physically, we're solid,' she acknowledged, unapologetic for the running commentary of her sex life in Scotland. 'But, whenever I try to have a meaningful conversation about our future, he just produces his chequebook and encourages me to buy something pretty.'

Despite her face paint, Zoë's distress was plain to see. Titty had to be the catalyst for change.

'All relationships entail peaks and troughs, highs and lows, ups and downs. You've never had a long-term relationship. Only flings. So you don't realise this is completely normal. Par for the course. The intensity of the first few months does fizzle out, it's impossible to sustain, but development doesn't mean degeneration. A relationship changes, that's all. You go through different phases, each one presents its own unique set of challenges, and staying committed is key. As Lady Rutherford would say, "the course of true love never did run smooth".'

'Surely you're not speaking from experience?' Zoë queried why her friend was a font of knowledge.

'Contrary to popular opinion, Roderick and I aren't the perfect couple.'

'Trouble in paradise?'

'No, nothing serious,' she backtracked. 'Just *les petits chagrins* as the French-speaker would say. A willingness to work through your problems as a couple is the foundation of a marriage.'

The women were poles apart. Chalk and cheese. But, no matter how much their lives diverged, opposites always attracted and Zoë trusted her judgment implicitly.

'Titty,' she ventured, 'I've made a stupid mistake. Will you be my maid of honour?'

CHAPTER 37

Charlotte did not unpack. Taxi still loaded with luggage, she entered the empty cottage, dragged her jet-lagged limbs up the stairs and hovered outside the baby's nursery.

John had restored it to spare room status while she plunged headfirst into Las Vegas-style oblivion. The crib was dismantled. The woodland animals had scurried away to happier homes. Baby gifts were either returned to owner or stacked in wooden boxes marked Charity Shop. It was a depressingly blank canvas.

'Madam?' the driver hooted.

'Five minutes.'

'Beware the meter's running.'

'Trust me, it's the least of my problems.'

Battling a hangover, Charlotte limped into the kitchen. In previous years, it sparkled with festive cheer, like a replica of Santa's grotto. But Christmas couldn't permeate this grief. She tore down the single forlorn strand of red tinsel encasing the calendar where John had crossed out the due date. Rearranged magnets on the fridge door that appeared naked without the baby scans. Wept over the heartfelt condolence cards on the windowsill.

Unable to muster the energy for gardening, Charlotte's beloved pots and plants were suffering in the icy slush dumped on the landscape by snowy clouds. She had failed to insulate the trays of winter bedding plants – forget-me-nots, primula, viola – from frost with bubblewrap and mesh. Her frost-bitten vegetable patch would produce no delights next year. Nor the plug pants which she'd neglected to store for safe-keeping in the shed. Sprays of lobelia had solidified like fountains of ice. The bird bath was frozen; the feeding table was empty; the tulip bulbs blown across the grass. A heron inspected the fallen leaves in the stream. She hadn't even pruned roses to prevent wind-rock or raised patio containers onto bricks to avoid them stewing in sludge like soldiers lumbered with trench foot in World War One.

Charlotte imagined her stepdaughter playing outside, making snow angels or riding her sleigh in the neighbouring fields or feeding the ponies in tartan winter coats on the next-door farm.

John's weekend had entailed a trip to Norfolk to tell his mother the sad news. He was due home soon. That meant the letter required urgent attention. The truth threatened to cause an irreparable rift in her family (hence the getaway vehicle to her sister's house) and repercussions for her job. But these scissors of honesty were the only way to free the victims entangled in her web of lies. She took off her engagement ring and put pen to paper.

Darling John, she began, *I have a medical condition...*

CHAPTER 38

Concluding a double shift, Titty wearily dispensed of her scrubs, brushed her hair up into a ponytail and changed into a striped polo shirt, navy corduroy trousers and comfortable loafers. Only a half-eaten banana remained in the on-call room's barren fruit bowl. Yawning, she yearned for a proper snack, some peace and quiet and silky cotton bed sheets. But her nightly duties weren't done.

ICU was deserted at 11 p.m. as she snuck into Oliver's cubicle. Amid the promotion, increased workload and Las Vegas trip, Titty had not visited for a while and was riven with remorse. She'd bought him a souvenir from her travels – a snow globe of Nevada tourist sites like the MGM casino, Bellagio, Hoover Dam – to compensate.

'Nurse,' she called, stumped by the empty bed, 'isn't it rather late to subject Oliver to tests?'

'I'm sorry,' the portly woman trudged towards her.

'Don't apologise,' Titty said, taking off her Barbour jacket, no time for grudges, 'just let me know when the doctors have finished their scans.'

'I wanted to call you, but it breached hospital ethics and I couldn't lose my job.'

'Hospital ethics?'

'The Professors Wedgewood-Beaverbrook are his legal next of kin,' she expounded. 'Their decision to withdraw the feeding tube was final.'

Terror immobilised Titty. No, no, no. This had to be a case of mistaken identity.

'Dr Wedgewood-Beaverbrook, your brother died earlier this evening.'

•

Dazed, Titty heard a door swing on its hinges and felt someone enclose her fingers around a warm paper cup. Courtesy of the brain's in-built shock absorber, she must have blacked out. Her elbow still throbbed from hitting the hard floor. There were vague recollections of staff manhandling her dead weight into the relatives' room. Now a man sat beside her on the stiff sofa.

'Roderick?' she hoped, but the Estuary English accent thwarted her theory.

'Zoë's in Berlin at a Christmas market,' Josh explained, 'so I took the hospital call and came straight here. The nurses dialled the first few numbers in your phone contacts.'

Instinctively turning away from the Abercrombie & Fitch tracksuited footballer, Titty shakily sipped her tea.

'Camomile,' she commented.

'Yes, it's good for shock. Dad drank urns of the stuff when mum passed away.'

Returning in dribs and drabs, memories of the events before Titty fainted took time for her to process.

'Oliver is dead?' she was disconnected from each word as if speaking a foreign language.

'That's right,' Josh nodded.

'When?'

'Last night.'

'Did he suffer?'

'No, the nurses said it was very peaceful.'

Putting their paper teacups on the end table, Josh gripped Titty's shoulder as she convulsed with sobs.

'Five years,' she wailed, detachment into despair as the pixelated picture suddenly gained frightening clarity. 'That's how long I've waited for Oliver to wake up. Five fucking years.

He can't be dead. I won't allow it. He's a fighter, a survivor. He can't be dead.'

'Titty...' Josh pulled her close.

'No,' the uptight doctor clung, bitterly, to her morals and fought off his comfort.

But Oliver was dead. Everything had changed. She curled into him and cried and cried and cried.

•

'You'd have liked Oliver.'

Josh smiled, indulgent, as he brewed another cup of camomile tea at the machine.

'Honestly,' Titty asserted, throat parched from crying a river of tears. 'Oliver wasn't a snob like me. He treated all his associates as equals. Paid no regard to their background. He didn't care if you worked as a stockbroker or a shop assistant. He had friends from all walks of life. Oliver was a down-to-Earth guy born into a family of pompous aristocrats. He lit up peoples' lives. He deserved more than to die alone on a hospital ward.'

Scrunching a damp tissue, she turned the key on the Las Vegas snow globe. *Luck be a Lady* played. It had never sounded so sad.

'Respectful of my parents,' she shared, 'I pledged a vow of silence, but Oliver supported Sunderland FC from a young age. I helped him stash their posters under his bed so the Professors wouldn't punish him and invent cover stories for him when he bunked off school to hitch a ride to wherever they had a match.'

'Why "The Black Cats"?' Josh polished his Nike hi-tops with a spare tissue.

'Back then, Sunderland was the underdog, low down in the Premier League. Oliver didn't want to support the top teams that had sold their soul to foreign owners who treated the clubs like a commercial brand not a brotherhood.'

'I expected him to be a rugby nut.'

'Oliver did captain the under-18s at Eton,' she admitted, 'but his main passion was football. After the surfing accident, I renewed his season ticket every year, unable to accept he would never watch another match.'

Titty paused to replay the past few hours. How could the Professors let Oliver starve to death without even telling her... Patients hailed the Professors miracle workers, a God send, but now she wondered if medicine was simply a conduit for their egos. The selflessness was actually deliberate self-deprecation. And investing thousands in their children's education wasn't just family tradition; it was to guarantee reflected glory in their retirement. Reflected glory. The same motivation for Roderick pushing her towards the promotion.

'Five years, four months and eighteen days,' she went on. 'Regardless of my parents' decisive action, the chances of Oliver recovering were infinitesimal. But I still thought he'd wake up.'

'Until the day she died,' Josh empathised, 'I still thought mum would beat cancer.'

Titty nodded.

'I just wish I could have said goodbye,' she disclosed the overriding sadness. 'Even if Oliver was completely unresponsive. I wanted to tell him I loved him for one last time. But Roderick's probably right, PVS patients are "zombies", and he didn't have a clue that I was by his side for five years.'

'I reckon he knew,' Josh said.

'Really?'

'I'm not a cardiologist, but I believe love's depends on the heart, not the brain, so there was no reason why he couldn't register the signals you were sending.'

Titty wiped her tears.

'Thanks for coming,' she stared, earnestly, at Josh who had been a pillar of support on a night when grief threatened to gnaw through her foundations.

'Anytime.'

'I owe you a new t-shirt,' she pointed at the tear-sodden shoulders of his Nike crew neck.

'Deal,' Josh agreed, nudging her knee, 'but I owe you something, too. An apology. In Scotland, I accused you of not having a heart. I was wrong.'

Titty hadn't forgotten the criticism.

'What made you change your mind?' she asked.

'Because, tonight, I watched it break.'

While Oliver met a premature end, Titty observed a new page of conciliation turned in this relationship.

'You're getting married in a week,' she said. 'Go home. Get some rest.'

'I'd rather be here.'

'But I'm sure Roderick's en route.'

'Titty, the nurse said he rejected the hospital's call.'

'Well,' she belligerently defended her emotionally illiterate fiancé. 'Maybe he's in court. Or driving.'

'At 3.30 a.m.?'

'Not inconceivable for a workaholic.'

Nurses had already parcelled Oliver's nautical possessions into cardboard boxes to clear the room for another unfortunate individual. His ship had sailed. Now they watched doctors wheel a teenager into the cubicle trailed by a woeful relative. Titty didn't wish their future on her worst enemy. Time made your heart inured to the pain but never immune.

'Life's too short for our betrayal to ruin our one chance at happiness,' she asserted.

Their spouses-to-be, momentarily demoted by Oliver's death, returned to the forefront of her thoughts.

'Roderick really makes you happy?' he questioned.

'He's Mr Perfect.'

'But is he perfect for you?'

'He has to be.'

For once, Josh did not capitalise on her floundering answers.

'Trust me,' he said, voice devoid of his trademark bravado and banter. 'Your secret's safe. I won't breathe a word.'

Grateful, Titty gave a sad smile, and promptly dissolved into tears at the ineffable loss of her brother, her ally, her best friend.

CHAPTER 39

Two ruby-nosed reindeer pulled the gilded gold carriage that delivered Zoë to her ostentatious white wedding. Ice sculptures of 20ft Norwegian spruces ornamented with a dazzling gold star and a cornucopia of Harry Winston diamond-encrusted baubles flanked the barn entrance. Inside existed a winter wonderland.

'It's beautiful,' she lingered in the shadows while Charlotte wove a white rose into her peroxide blonde plaited up-do that showed off ribbons of diamond earrings.

Lanterns dangled from oak beams in the gabled roof. Pews garnished with sprays of white orchids, dove feathers and crystals accommodated guests in obligatory all-white ensembles. A celebrity harpist played Wagner's The Bridal March from a podium crafted out of white-frosted pine cones as Zoë began her graceful ascent along a carpet of powdered snow towards the altar.

Gently lifting her friend's bridal train, Charlotte welled-up. Hopes of her own wedded bliss lay in tatters. John had stormed into her sister's house, thrown her confession into the fire and ended their engagement, angrily suggesting she sought professional help for her addiction to lying. Though in a barn of two-hundred people, she felt so alone, desperate, grieving the partnership she had lost.

Zoë waved, snootily, at socialites in fur stoles who were miffed they hadn't bagged the eligible footballer and at Charlotte and Titty wearing white meringue puffball dresses.

Her ample assets burst forth from the beaded lace bodice with each step. The front row belonged to magazine photographers hustling to get the best shot. Then Josh's white three-piece silk wedding suit with red rose boutonnière manifested at the altar.

'Dearly beloved,' the registrar introduced guests to the ceremony.

Beside the bride, Titty clasped a crystal bouquet of poinsettia and snowdrops, concertedly avoiding Josh's gaze. And his England football ball cufflinks that made Roderick, her begrudging plus-one, wince with bad taste.

'First, I am required to ask anyone here present who knows a reason why these persons may not lawfully marry, to declare it now.'

During the tense pause, Zoë swore time ground to a halt. Milliseconds felt longer than Mesozoic eras. All a dangerous opportunity for her fraudulent history to interfere with the present. But no dirt was dug up and the traditional vows were the stepping stones to their future.

To have and to hold
From this day forward
For better, for worse,
For richer, for poorer,
In sickness and in health,
To love and to cherish,
Till death do you part

'Do you, Zoë, take Josh to be your lawfully wedded husband?'

'I do.'

'Do you, Josh, take Zoë to be your lawfully wedded wife?'

'I do.'

'You may exchange the rings,' the registrar said, and Titty and Pete proffered platinum wedding bands. 'I now pronounce you man and wife.'

Kissing to ebullient applause, Zoë's reef knots of stress unwound. Access to Josh's fortune was guaranteed as per conditions of the pre-nup. Unassailable, the charm offensive was over. But, she realised, marrying the love of her life provided the ultimate satisfaction.

'Toss the bouquet!' the congregation bellowed.

Charlotte inadvertently caught the £1,000 masterpiece which she hurriedly offloaded to Josh's eager niece who exploded with joy.

'Congratulations,' Roderick shook hands with the groom.

'Thanks, mate.'

'What a wonderful service,' Titty complimented, hugging the couple, snuffing out a tiny spark of affection as Josh's lips skimmed hers.

Sophie's absence was the snowball that triggered an avalanche – WAG after WAG had abandoned the wedding to banish winter blues in the southern hemisphere – and Zoë appreciated her friends' loyalty.

'I couldn't have asked for a better maid-of-honour,' she pulled Titty closer for a photograph.

'My pleasure.'

Guests showered the Rockinghams with fluttery white confetti as they frolicked in the aisle like love-sick teenagers and emerged from the barn into a crisp winter day to pose for photographs. Behind, male and female Olympic figure skaters in purple velvet and rhinestones performed a jump sequence on the ice rink. A slide chassé into a twizzling synchronised triple axel was capped by an impressive death-spiral where the man anchored his toe pick like a pivot and his partner spun 360^0 perilously close to the slippery surface. The finale was a flurry of criss-cross skating as they carved *Zosh: Together Forever* into the ice.

•

A fleet of pink helicopters chopped the sky slowly filling with graphite grey snow clouds to deliver hand-picked individuals for the wedding party held in the adjoining Milking Parlour reconfigured as a palace of ice.

From the wrought-iron chandelier, a giant crystal lovebird swooped over the constellation of ice tables strewn with gold petals, icicles aglow with white candles and gold-dusted acorns. Two urns of mulled wine heralded the rectangular top table where Josh and Zoë packed on the PDAs while Pete, his best-man, stood to make a speech to the star-studded audience.

'May I interrupt,' Zoë apprehended the microphone from the bewildered best-man. 'At risk of making my mascara run, I'd like to recite a Shakespeare sonnet that encapsulates how I feel about Josh. P.S. I discovered this text while snooping in Lady Rutherford's library at the castle late one night when she had gone to bed. Sorry Roderick.'

'Glad to be of help,' he smiled, though secretly hatched a law suit to bring the trespasser to justice.

Usually a lover of lights, camera and action, unfamiliar butterflies caused havoc as Zoë felt nerves about public speaking for the first time since her GCSE English oral.

'Let me not to the marriage of true minds admit impediments,' Zoë began, timid, the pages rattling in her hands.

But, she realised, this was a challenge. No different from doing 100 m.p.h. on the motorway. Or her attempt to climb Kilimanjaro with Oliver. Trusty adrenalin kicked in and she resumed with a theatrical cough.

'Love is not love which alters when it alteration finds, Or bends with the remover to remove: O no! it is an ever-fixed mark that looks on tempests and is never shaken; It is the star to every wandering bark, whose worth's unknown, although his height be taken. Love's not Time's fool, though rosy lips and cheeks within his bending sickle's compass come: Love alters not with his brief hours and weeks, But bears it out even to the edge of doom. If this be error and upon me proved, I never writ, nor no man ever loved.'

The misty-eyed congregation clapped and Josh cued dapper waiters to present the elaborate appetiser – salmon gravadlax with champagne mustard – followed by roast goose with chestnut stuffing. Zoë had subscribed to a strict pre-wedding detox. A nine-day all-liquid diet involving protein shakes made from powdered egg and gallons of water. She wolfed down the solids.

'Please note they're not geese from the grounds of your castle,' Josh joked, loosening his Windsor-knotted tie.

'Geese?' Roderick was incredulous. 'It's far too common a bird to be found anywhere on the Rutherford estate.'

Haughtily, he sniffed his wine, a festive blend of cloves, cinnamon and nutmeg, able to detect the specific Italian red.

'Not a fan of Chianti?' Zoë assumed.

'Ugh, no…'

'It's marvellously rich,' Titty averted an argument and ladled more into their glasses.

Make-up smudged, Charlotte was crying into her wine as she watched young guests play hide-and-seek.

'John hates me,' she sighed, despondently picking at the meat on her snowflake-shaped plate.

'Losing a child takes its toll on all couples,' Titty gratefully accepted the vegetarian nut roast.

'He blocks my calls.'

'Time apart to process your emotions is healthy.'

'He's changed the locks to the cottage.'

'Be patient.'

'It's entirely my fault.'

'Stillbirth is no reflection on the mother. If anyone is to blame in this situation, it's John. I've tried to tolerate his moodiness, but you need his unequivocal support while you and your cope with the loss. If Dr Bishop's bereavement counselling isn't helping, I can put you in contact with a colleague at *Liverpool General*. Dr Upton, he's very senior. I have the clout to expedite your referral.'

'Titty, listen to me.'

'I am.'

'No, you're exonerating me. I've been trying to tell you the truth for weeks. It was a phantom pregnancy. I didn't miscarry.'

Clocking her wine glass, Titty automatically did a series of mental contortions to calculate the number of refills.

'I'm not drunk,' Charlotte committed to a confession, 'and I'm not delusional with post-traumatic stress. I'm infertile.'

On that bombshell, dessert was served. Children devoured the winter pudding bombe and chatted to journalists interviewing them for quotes and captions to accompany the magazine article.

Josh brandished a forkful of chilled berry cheesecake swirled in vanilla ice cream. Zoë licked the luxuriant dessert with crème de cassis straight off his cutlery. Worries about fitting her Melissa Odabash honeymoon bikinis melted just like if she exposed this palace of ice to a blowtorch. Sophie's melon cake was untouched in the corner.

An X-Factor girl group, attired in skimpy elf costumes, infused Santa Baby with sex appeal. The extroverted happy couple didn't hesitate to hit the dancefloor amidst puffs of dry ice. Under a disco ball, Josh and Zoë spontaneously recreated the famous Dirty Dancing lift while a video montage of their courtship, an idea stolen from the wedding fayre, was projected above the top table where Charlotte slumped like a lonely singleton.

'John, it's me, again,' she left another voice-message. 'Please call me back. I couldn't convey the extent of my regret in a letter.'

As she wallowed in wine and self-pity, Josh performed the caterpillar dance move and Zoë waxed lyrical about his fit physique to *Ok!* reporters. Charlotte knew the vanity was a façade. Lust had evolved into love.

'Care to dance?' Roderick returned from a work call.

'Um...' Titty was still reeling from the news that her friend had sunken to such deceitful depths.

'You're pale.'

'Oh, really?'

'Hospitals are breeding grounds for germs. You've probably caught something. The bloody winter nova virus has incapacitated half my legal team which has multiplied my workload. It'll be a Christmas miracle if I honour your family's invitation to Klosters.'

'But it's an annual tradition...'

'The victims of the Taiwanese tsunami need me more than the slopes of Switzerland.'

This week, Titty realised, there'd been one wedding and a funeral. Oliver was deprived of a big day. Kids. A chance to grow old. But she still had a life to live, a marriage to plan, and there wasn't a moment to waste on pointless arguments.

'Let's dance,' she took Roderick's hand.

The aristocrat waltzed Titty into a fallaway whisk, a re-enactment of their graduation ball dance, before bringing her upright for a tender embrace.

'I can't wait to make you Lady Rutherford,' he declared.

Swaying in sync to the music, her engagement ring no longer felt the equivalent of a noose around her neck. Then Titty stopped dead as if shot by a stun gun. Motion images of her steamy tryst with Josh unfolded above the table. One by one, guests registered the live drama.

'Turn it off,' she wriggled out of Roderick's arms to grapple with the projector. 'Off. Off.'

But the damage was done. Zoë turned whiter than her wedding dress. Eyes darting from one traitor to the other.

'What the hell…?' Roderick stuttered, flailing, no legal precedent to inform his behaviour.

'You bastard!' Titty was furious that she had been duped into believing Josh was capable of integrity.

'It was an accident,' he pleaded innocence. 'Rockingham Palace's security tapes and Zoë's phone footage must have got jumbled on my computer. I totally forgot about the cameras. I swear that I didn't even know there was a video of us.'

Ashamed, Josh approached his wife, but she was fleeing the disaster zone, chased by reporters hungry for indignity.

The three corners of this wretched love triangle filtered out to the courtyard framed by potted white birch trees with Swarovski star adornments that doubled as pendants for guests to take home. Hotel residents toasting marshmallows in the fire pit were befuddled by the bride who tore off her veil, impervious to flakes of snow starting to fall, and looked heavenward for answers to this impossibly awful end to her wedding that was the explosive conclusion of a year's worth of white lies.

'It was a terrible mistake,' Titty begged. 'A one-night stand. A massive error in judgment. We were drunk, sozzled, plastered. Three sheets to the wind. Smashed.'

Clocking up decades of alcohol abuse, Zoë understood the concept, but wasn't swayed by endless synonyms.

'Consensual sex,' she insisted, 'doesn't happen unless you want it.'

Speckled by snow, Zoë suddenly became acutely aware of her surroundings. Of the hotel residents, guests, photographers, journalists. This was her wedding day. It couldn't be remembered for all the wrong reasons, sabotaged by scandal. She had to be magnanimous to rescue herself from utter humiliation.

'So,' Zoë stared at them, 'you're adamant it meant nothing? No feelings attached? Just sex?'

'Yes, of course,' Titty rushed to confirm.

The cameras turned to her husband.

'Josh,' she repeated, 'it meant nothing?'

The footballer didn't reply. Guests including Charlotte who braved the blizzard for a front-row view were staggered. Titty felt outraged how the bastard could toy with their emotions at such a crucial moment.

'Josh's lying,' she exclaimed. 'He thrives on drama. Laps up the attention. Ignore him.'

Zoë shook her head with solemn realisation.

'No, he's the only one telling the truth.'

CHAPTER 40

Valentine's Day

2 months later

Charlotte

The influx of hoity-toity parents driving vehicles inappropriate for suburban Cheshire caused a mile-long traffic jam and horns blared from angry residents waiting an eternity to reverse out of their homes.

Charlotte's hatchback was dwarfed by black Range Rovers as she parallel parked in the residential street.

'Excuse me,' she wended a path through mothers gossiping outside the assembly hall where the concert was staged.

Each February, virtuosos at Roe House were selected to perform for the town mayor in this curved auditorium of Italianate architecture with ornate pedimented windows, a square cupola and encircled by a terracotta mosaic frieze.

Charlotte snuck past the organist to grab a chair in the back row of the tiered grandstand. All around, pushy parents videotaped their kids to scrutinise their technique. She was wowed by the range of operatic and orchestral pieces wowed, particularly by Chloe's violin solo that concluded the event. Her J.S. Bach: Concerto in E major received a standing ovation before parents following Horatia's lead targeted teachers for updates on their musical prodigies.

'John!' Charlotte called, locating him at the refreshments table, making chit-chat with other dads.

He looked much healthier than their last encounter. More rested. The dark under-eye circles were less pronounced.

'Please don't hurry away,' she implored, hands in the prayer position. 'I just need a minute.'

A couple of snooty prefects crunching batons of celery, cucumber, carrot and red pepper served with hummus or an animal-free soya cream cheese stared at Charlotte whose spotty duffel coat and bobble hat suggested she wasn't from these posh parts.

'Leave me and my daughter alone,' he demanded.

'I'm not here to make problems.'

She realised inveigling his daughter's recital was sneaky. But she had to convey the life-changing news.

'So you're here to offer another pathetic apology?' he referenced the innumerable grovelling messages on his voice mail.

'Not exactly.'

'leave me alone.'

'John, I'm pregnant.'

'As if,' he chortled, picking up a pitted black olive, not entertaining the idea that she was carrying his child.

'Believe it or not,' she insisted, 'I'm telling the truth.'

'You're a compulsive liar. You conned me, your friends and family, and everyone at *Brooklands Primary* for nearly nine months. Christ, you even made Chloe think her baby brother had died.'

'The doctor did a thorough examination,' she persisted, unveiling a scan which John instantly dismissed.

'Did you get a 2-for-1 deal at the same fake hospital?'

'No, it's from *Liverpool General*. I've reached ten weeks. Everything appears normal.'

Draining his cup of water, John sat on the edge of the table to consider he might become a dad for the second time.

'You're pregnant?' he grasped the scan.

'Yes.'

'Oh God.'

'I know.'

'Was your infertility a lie, too?'

'Absolutely not.'

Hoping for an antidepressants prescription after her break-up, Charlotte's jaw had dropped when the doctor revealed that a bun was in the oven. She visited five different GPs for confirmation. And Titty's Harley Street obstetrician who charged £200 per appointment.

'Ten weeks?' he verified.

'Yep.'

'Just after the "stillbirth"?'

'Yep.'

Their sporadic sex life ensured any lovemaking was put firmly on the map of memories. This intimate occurrence, the first since Charlotte was able to take off the chastity belt, had been a passionate fusion, each partner hungry for comfort after the harrowing news.

'John,' she said, 'it's a medical miracle. This baby is real. I don't expect you to forgive me. But I am going to raise your child. Whether or not I have to do it alone.'

Eagle-eyed, Horatia spotted them and rushed to interfere. To whip up a tornado of trouble, Charlotte could have outed the ex-wife's bullying, but she chose not to sink to that level. She stoically withstood the abuse.

'This wicked stepmother shouldn't be near children,' the financier accused, poised to alert security. 'A predatory female like you ought to be on the child-abuser register. Chloe is scarred for life by your manipulation.'

The vixen in a black suit draped a proprietary arm around her lover like the tendril of a praying mantis. Charlotte ached from the indication she had wormed her way back into his affections. But John forcibly removed it.

'Charlotte wiped our daughter's tears when you made her cry,' he was brutally honest.

'Darling…'

'Horatia, the least you can do is leave us to speak in private.'

Stroppy, Horatia pivoted on her thin heel and went to fraternise with the headmaster.

'If the pregnancy is true,' he said, excitement tempered by niggling doubts, 'I want to be involved.'

'Of course.'

'Are you still at your sister's?'

'Yes.'

'Please keep in touch.'

'I will.'

'You do realise,' John confirmed, a poignant footnote, 'that I'd never have abandoned you for suffering from endometriosis. I wanted more kids, undeniably, but I wanted you more.'

A spotlight shone on the sad irony, Charlotte nodded and accidentally bumped into Chloe as she returned to the car.

'Your performance was terrific,' her stepmother praised.

'Thank you.'

'I can't fathom how you make five strings sound so melodic.'

'Practice, practice, practice.'

Head down, the girl had obviously been warned by Horatia to deny her existence. But she was blessed with John's compassion. After a beat, Chloe made a bashful admission.

'I miss you, Charlotte.'

'Me, too.'

'Mummy's cupcakes don't compare to yours.'

Charlotte smiled.

'Oh, Chloe, I'm so sorry for hurting you.'

'It's okay. Even grown-ups make silly mistakes sometimes.'

'Yes, we do.'

They hugged.

'Rushford Lodge,' Charlotte flaunted a leaflet. 'It's an activity centre used by Girl Guides in the Lake District. Archery, badminton, horse riding. There's loads of fun on offer. If you ever fancy a trip, let me know. But don't tell your mother.'

Titty

2320: patient is alert and responsive post-angioplasty...

Titty updated the notes, filed the report and polished her stethoscope.

'Any special plans?' the bubbly night-shift nurse made a casual inquiry.

'Plans?'

'For Valentine's Day.'

'I hadn't realised.'

'No hot date?'

'Unlikely,' she glanced, dejectedly, at the heart garland above the nurses' station.

Avoiding embarrassing questions about her relationship status, Titty disappeared up the fire escape to the roof. Since working in *Portsmouth Hospital*, it was a familiar spot. Nippy, even in her padded Moncler coat, but nice to get away from the hospital's recycled air.

No new messages

The glutton for punishment confirmed the Wedgewood-Beaverbrooks hadn't extended an olive branch. Not even a paltry twig. The scandalous end to Titty's engagement meant she was excised like a malignant tumour and thrown in the bin of medical waste without a second thought. With insulting speed, a Dutch UN negotiator, daughter of an old family friend, filled the slot of Roderick's fiancée. Her parents acted as if she'd never been born. So much for two stalwarts of the so-called "caring profession".

Ugh, she sighed, aware Oliver would have been a guaranteed ally during this Cold War.

'How things change,' Titty reflected on the past riotous year.

Twelve months ago, she boarded the rollercoaster in Paris, accepting a marriage proposal ticket. Last summer, she loosened its screws with her betrayal. Now, the ride broken, she waded through its debris all alone. But the most disconcerting section of track had been discovering she'd never loved Roderick and her confidence was greater without the egotistical aristocrat. She missed Charlotte and Zoë more than she missed her mother.

Titty had fled *Liverpool General* to Portsmouth because it was Oliver's stomping ground during his spell as a registrar. Every lonely night, she pinpointed landmarks from her brother's postcards. The Spinnaker Tower, Isle of Wight ferry terminal, P&O cruise ships.

Celebrity magazines kept her abreast of Zoë's saga. Minutes after marrying, she filed for divorce – the "hip and happening" couple had turned into the "has-beens" that hardly were – but the WAG had become reclusive in recent weeks. If the pre-nup was declared nul and void, Titty feared destitution was her fate.

```
Following     Dr     Wedgewood-Beaverbrook's
resignation,  Liverpool  General  Hospital  is
pleased  to  appoint  Dr Richard Lam, 36, as the
newest cardiology consultant.
```

To get a transfer to Portsmouth, Titty had to accept a demotion. She now endured Richard Lam's smug face on the cover of the *BMJ* app on her iPhone. Professor Wedgewood-Beaverbrook refused to exert any influence in this neck of the woods. She was back to being a registrar. Here, the only way up the career ladder was hard work, not heritage, which had been a shock to the system, but she was determined to prove to Dr Lam that merit would take her to the top.

In lieu of consultant commitments, Titty was graced with time to do some unorthodox research. Scientifically, she'd been trained to recognise the brain as the epicentre of emotion. Yet thousands upon thousands of years of history said it was the heart. In Chinese medicine, the heart was seen as the centre of shén. Aristotle isolated the heart as the organ that ruled our response to the world. Its historical interpretation influenced the Christian devotion to the Sacred Heart of Jesus and it had been a feature of the lexicon for centuries, used in books, films, poetry. Maybe it was a fallacy, or a fairy story to boost sales of Valentine's Day cards, roses and literotica, but Titty had gained a new perspective on the organ she'd studied for so long.

Right now, hers was still broken in half by her brother's death. It made scattering his ashes a daunting prospect.

Delaying the moment for months, she'd designated tonight as Oliver's final farewell and produced the wooden receptacle from her handbag. She'd chosen Portsmouth for obvious reasons. It was the UK's naval base and main shipping channel with cruise liners and warships including HMS Illustrious docked in the harbour. This was where the buccaneering action-man felt most at home.

'Safe journey,' she whispered, throwing the urn's contents into the wind that carried them to the sea below.

'Titty?'

A voice made her jump, there was never normally anyone else up here except for seagulls and she turned to find Josh emerging from the roof hatch. They hadn't spoken since the wedding. The coach almost dropped him from the team, and he almost lost his advertising deal with Lynx, but both were too enamoured with his star status to punish the misdemeanours in his personal life.

'Sorry to startle you,' he approached.

'Why are you here?' Titty gasped, instantly critical of his shiny suit worn with white trainers.

'Liverpool played a match in Portsmouth tonight. We won. I came direct from the post-match press conference.'

For a nanosecond, Titty was disappointed that his first words weren't a proclamation of love, but she wouldn't feed the monster inside that made her wonder if the flash footballer was a better match for her than a landed aristocrat.

'You should be on the coach home,' Titty turned away with decisive body language.

'I've been searching for you since the wedding,' Josh remained on the roof like a bad smell. '*Liverpool General* wouldn't release any contact details. I tried Roderick. He gave me a black eye. And your parents hung up on all my calls.'

'So, who did you bribe for information?' she vowed to unfriend the mole.

'A nurse on the ICU ward remembered me from Oliver's death and waived some of the security protocol.'

'How could you lie to Zoë?' she interrupted, still mystified by his behaviour.

'Lie to her?'

'Yes, you told her that our mistake meant something. Your careless actions ruined everything. Her wedding day. My relationship. Your reputation.'

'Titty,' he stepped in. 'I'm desperately sorry for the pain I caused, but I should never have married Zoë.'

'Why on Earth not?'

'Because I'd fallen in love with her best friend.'

Titty shook her head, unable to believe the footballer could be genuine, and Josh walked closer and closer, pinning her against the safety railings until she was forced to confront his confession.

'I love you,' he repeated, blue eyes penetrating hers like laser beams of intent, 'and I know you feel the same way about me.'

'No…'

'You accuse me of lying when it's you who won't admit the truth.'

'No…'

Titty was flailing in his stare.

'All we do is argue,' she protested.

'Not entirely.'

'You know what I mean.'

'Yes. In the past two months, my life has been so much quieter without you. No driving me crazy with your posh pronunciation, making mountains out of molehills, football-bashing. But I don't want a quiet life. I miss having a sparring partner. I miss everything about you.'

'We're worlds apart,' she railed against the sentimental slush.

'Worlds can collide.'

'No…'

'I understand it's scary. The moment of impact is a real shock. But I'll protect you from any pain.'

Titty felt a tear trickle down her face.

'I love you,' he wiped it away. 'I'm not Mr Perfect in any way, shape or form, but I might be perfect for you.'

Josh seized her shaking body, and they kissed passionately, before she severed the embrace and ran down the fire escape stairs as if running from a real inferno.

Zoë

When Josh cheated, WAGs tongues were set wagging and Sophie even jetted back from the Bahamas. But not to dry her tears. Simply to get their names in the news with all sorts of salacious lies that reduced Zoë's reputation to rubble.

One pair of pristine Christian Louboutin stilettos, she typed, laptop balanced on a pile of taxidermied lovebirds that Sophie had neglected to burn in the store cupboard where she'd been holed up since the wedding. *Colour: patent leopard-print. Size: adult 7. Heel height: 140mm.*

'Sold,' she accepted the highest bid.

A once-worn Hervé Leger bejewelled bandage dress, she uploaded the next item. *Colour: aubergine. Size: adult XS (but slightly strained in the midriff area). Sleeveless. Concealed back zipper.*

Each sale was agonising, like auctioning off a child, but this one hurt more than most. She'd worn the £690 spandex/nylon/rayon masterpiece exactly a year ago, on Valentine's Day, the night she got engaged.

The dress sold within minutes. Zoë was fast racking up a profit even if they were sold at knock-down prices. Due to its brevity, the marriage was annulled, not ended in divorce, but Josh had agreed to honour the original terms of their pre-nup. Technically, she was minted with enough wonga to open a Swiss bank account. But she'd returned the engagement ring and wouldn't accept a penny from the traitor and had resorted to selling *Zoë's Zone* stock (and half her wardrobe) on *eBay*.

Yuk, she said, stretching her with a walk out to the shop floor, scowling at the décor that she'd always hated.

Knock. Knock.

Damn, couldn't the person read the NO VISITORS sign? Even the postman knew to keep his distance as if there were a rabid dog on the premises.

'Go away!'

Knock. Knock.

'Aargh, who is it?'

'Margot.'

Zoë paused, concerned it was a reporter impersonating her former friend as a mean trick. She peered through the blackout curtains where journalists camped on the pavement for exclusive pictures of her meltdown. It really was Margot. And she was back to her va va voom best, proving 70 was the new 50 in a black lace top, purple rah-rah skirt and fingerless gloves.

'What do you want?' Zoë called.

'Just to talk.'

'No, Margot, please go.'

'Zoë, I'm quite possibly the only person out here who cares about you. Please let me in. I'm on your side.'

Inch by inch, she undid the padlocks worthy of guarding a vault in Fort Knox and opened the door.

'Oh, dear,' Margot deplored the dressed-down version of her surrogate daughter.

Slovenly in a slub t-shirt and joggers, dark roots crawled from the parting in Zoë's unkempt hair and her muscle mass had become fat thanks to weeks of ordering-in Chinese takeaways and scavenging for biscuits and cakes.

'I really loved Josh,' she broke down, fingering the Tiffany heart pendant *ZF* and *JR* clasped around her neck that she couldn't contemplate selling.

'I know, honey.'

'He was my fiancé and that bitch was my best friend.'

'I know.'

'They betrayed me.'

'Come here, honey, let's hug it out.'

Zoë savoured the human contact, hugging Margot's curves with all her strength, but she didn't deserve sympathy from the woman she'd humiliated.

'I was so horrible to you,' she wept.

'Honey, we all make mistakes when we're young and desperate to fit in. When I was a girl, my mother sent me to a convent school. The sisters made me cut my hair very short. Knowing it would please my mother, I agreed. But they also cut off my freedom of expression and creativity. I got expelled after less than six months. Thankfully, my hair grew back, except for a tiny section underneath which serves to remind me never to be so willing to conform.'

Feasting on the red velvet Valentine's Day tarts that Margot had brought from a bakery, they belted out *I Will Survive* and let bygones be bygones.

'I know what'll cheer you up,' the pensioner smiled. 'A make-over with all the bells and whistles.'

'I'm not in the mood.'

'Not for you,' she corrected. 'For *Zoë's Zone*. Black and white is so depressing.'

Ransacking the store cupboard for instruments, Margot found scissors and a hammer in the DIY box and channelled her inner vandal. Most of the rails were empty, stock sold, but she sliced all remaining monochrome garments into unrecognisable rags. She drew smiley faces on the oriental prints of brooding Buddhas and Shih Tzus; upturned the Bonsai trees in black buckets and smashed the sleek mirrors into smithereens. With a forceful blow, she beheaded the pretentious mannequins and splashed pink paint onto the geometric wallpaper like a girly graffiti artist.

'Ha ha,' Zoë laughed, such a rarity since the wedding that dust had gathered in her laughter lines. 'It's so gorgeous. Doesn't matter, though. I'm still selling the shop.'

'What?' Margot exclaimed, grinding soil into the black hardwood floor.

'With a boycott on WAGs, it will rise to oblivion once again. I can't afford the overheads. At least this divorce drama has given me a degree in common sense.'

'Well...' Margot schemed, 'I've had a bit of a windfall. Last year, in NYC, I bought a few shares in an up-and-coming internet company. Only a few hundred quid for fun. Out of the blue, I got a letter updating me on their value. The company's worth had skyrocketed. All shareholders were entitled to massive dividends. I made millions.'

'Fucking hell.'

'I could go into business with you. Even Stevens. 50% a piece.'

'I don't know…'

'Fashion is your forte,' Margot beseeched. 'Don't let those nasty WAGs win. You can't give up.'

'The store wasn't a success when I was in creative control.'

'Because you were still trying to replicate designer brands. If I was your business partner, I'd encourage you to flex your creative muscles at the sewing machine. Invent trends, don't copy them. Be a trailblazer.'

Arm twisted, Zoë grinned, showing her full set of glow-in-the-dark teeth, and realised her future wasn't so bleak with Margot's glitz and glamour.

'Before the relaunch,' the OAP said, 'I reckon you should take a holiday.'

'A holiday?'

'Yes, it's been a long, cold winter. Go and get some R&R in Hawaii. Make use of the honeymoon suite. I'll pay.'

'On one condition.'

'What?' Margot asked.

'You come with me.'

EPILOGUE

Like an unwritten rule in festival law, Glastonbury was a wash-out. A month's worth of rain fell in five hours on this Saturday in late June. Fields became seas, tents floating in the flood plains, music fans marooned on tiny islands of higher ground. Most Brits kept calm and carried on except for some who decided to treat the deluged Gloucestershire countryside as a water park by clambering up scaffolding to the top of the Pyramid Stage and sliding down into a pool of rain.

'Aargh!' Zoë cried with pain.

The pool was actually a puddle. Shallow, she'd slammed her foot against the hard ground. Now a steward was directing her to the medical hut and she hobbled, one Hunter wellington on and one off, through hippy communes and anoraked crowds.

'Hello again, Miss Hornby,' Dr Kent recognised her as the ringleader for a series of daft escapades during this five-day festival.

'I've broken my foot.'

'Doing what?'

'Aquaplaning.'

'How sensible.'

Zoë pouted.

'Well,' he checked his clipboard, 'there's a queue, so take a ticket and wait your turn.'

Irked by the delay, she borrowed a pair of crutches and followed his instructions.

'Number 92?' she read out in exclamation.

'Unfortunately, we're understaffed because half the workforce is trying to combat the flood,' Dr Kent pointed to a group of people scooping up buckets of sodden mud. 'The wet weather is hazardous. Unlike you, loads of people are skidding and sliding by accident which means an increase of twists and sprains and fractures requiring medical attention.'

Coquettish, Zoë batted her purple, blue and green lids that tapered into lightning bolt face paint decoration.

'I'm sure a handsome doctor like you is able to make an exception for a damsel in distress like me,' she felt Dr Kent's bicep through his scrub top.

'We operate on a first-come-first-serve basis,' he reprimanded.

'But I could die before Number 92 is called.'

'Nobody's ever died of a broken toe.'

'Well, then, I might die from the pain.'

'Take two of these,' he handed her aspirin tablets, sapped of enthusiasm for his job by the dare devils that stretched the hut's resources with their absurd antics.

•

Standing like a flamingo to ease the pressure on her injury, Zoë waited and waited and waited a while longer.

The past two hours in the medical hut exposed her to life in all its eclectic forms – the good, the bad and the ugly – and the full gamut of ailments that befell Glastonites. She struck up conversation with a emo drunk on cheap cider who'd contracted an STD from an unsavoury indie musician and mocked teenage pop-rockers from Swansea whose faulty cooking apparatus in their water-logged tent had left them with food-poisoning. Others, the walking wounded, were bruised and bloodied thanks to foolhardy stunts posted on social media. They looked like extras from a horror film who had stumbled off set still in costume and make-up.

'Number 92?' a nurse appeared from the triage area just as Zoë was on the brink of blowing a gasket.

'Me, me, me.'

'Okay, a doctor will see you now.'

'Thank the lord.'

Aspirin wearing off, she oohed and aahed into the curtained cubicle. Zoë. Titty. The estranged friends, now doctor and patient, stared at each other in disbelief.

'What the hell are you doing here?' Zoë was apoplectic.

'Voluntary work.'

'Voluntary?' she questioned the word.

'Yep.'

'But you swore never to come back to this mosh pit.'

'A lot's changed since we first met.'

In rare agreement, Zoë nodded.

'You're injured?' Titty's eyes were drawn to her swollen foot where blood mottled the nails of several manicured toes that were bent at obtuse angles.

'I slid off the Pyramid Stage roof. An amateurish attempt to impress a musician. I've broken at least one bone.'

'Hop up,' she levelled the bed, 'and let's take a closer look.'

'No chance,' Zoë protested, feeling a mishmash of coloured dye run down her cheeks from her milkmaid braid of rainbow-chalked hair that had got soaked. 'I don't want your help. I don't want you anywhere near me or my foot.'

Hurt, Titty's throat clogged with a lump of sadness.

'All my colleagues are busy,' she struggled to get the words out.

'Then I'll wait another two hours until one becomes free.'

Dragging the drip, Zoë prepared to stagger back to the chaotic waiting area, but a sharp twinge in her toes that'd turned from red to grey made her reconsider.

'Fine,' she growled, 'you can be my doctor. But make it quick.'

Attired in scrubs, Titty examined the injury, apologising for pressing on sore points, and arranged a portable X-ray.

'As predicted, you've broken your hallux.'

'My what?'

'Big toe. It's a nasty break. You won't need surgery, but I'll have to realign the bone. The other two toes have minor fractures and will heal without intervention.'

In preparation, Titty injected local anaesthetic to numb the area, but Zoë prepared for any possible shrieks of pain by stuffing a wad of surgical gauze between her teeth.

'Ready?' Titty checked.

'Mmm.'

'Three, two, one...'

Dr Wedgewood-Beaverbrook expertly straightened the wayward toe and wrapped it in a supportive cast.

'Use the crutches for six to eight weeks so you can avoid putting weight on it,' she advised.

'Damn,' Zoë hated being incapacitated.

'Sorry.'

'Will you stop apologising?'

'Sorry.'

Both cracked a smile.

'How are you?' Zoë asked.

'Okay.'

'Me, too.'

'Charlotte tells me that *Zoë's Zone* is flourishing.'

'Most of the glamorous grannies returned after I posted a written apology in the Cheshire Chronicle and I scored a few extra Brownie points by launching an anti "body-shaming" campaign on social media.'

'Yes, I signed it.'

'I deleted your name.'

'Oh.'

'Margot handles *Zoë's Zone* finances, marketing and accounts and I concentrate on design. Hand-sowing and stitching each garment that we sell has become the boutique's USP. Customers have responded very positively, happy to hear none of the clothes come from a sweat shop in Outer Mongolia. We've made a profit for the first time.'

Zoë popped another pain-killer and explained the crochet waistcoat, crop top and cut-off denim shorts with chunky leather belt à la Sienna Miller were components of her festival wear range.

'I hear Roderick ended your engagement,' she probed.

'Yes,' Titty said. 'He married Pandora von Beek, daughter of Dutch nobility, at *Rutherford Castle* a few weeks ago.

Exactly the ceremony and reception that Lady Philippa planned for us down to the asparagus soup starter. Tatler reports they're on honeymoon at his family's Antibes villa.'

'Oh, well, maybe the mosquitoes will make life difficult for them like they did for you.'

'Here's hoping.'

They paused.

'I can't believe it's been six years since we met in the queue for the toilets just over there.'

'It's as if fate brought us back together.'

'Not fate,' Charlotte hoiked back the curtain. 'Me.'

Both women gasped at their friend in full 1970s flower-power costume with a floral headband made from daisies and petunias and violas, gypsy maxidress floating over her 8-month baby bump and chunky sandals.

'I wondered why you kept encouraging me to drive all the way from Portsmouth to volunteer at this particular location,' Titty gasped.

'And why you got so excited when I booked tickets,' Zoë added her side of the story.

'Sorry to be sneaky, but I knew you, Zoë, wouldn't agree to meet Titty otherwise.'

'Too right,' the fashionista said. 'I don't like surprises unless they come in jewellery boxes. I'm outta here.'

Once again, she determined to leave, but Charlotte kept the crutches out of reach so the friends could resolve their rift. She seized their hands and placed them on her precious cargo. The baby kicked and Titty felt the swell of broodiness that Roderick had suppressed.

'I don't want this baby's two godmothers to be at loggerheads,' Charlotte. 'All three of us made terrible mistakes last year. That period in our lives proved men come and go. In the festival spirit of making love not war, I beg you to end this feud so our friendship doesn't disintegrate like our relationships did.'

A week earlier, Zoë had visited *Rockingham Palace*, the first time since the annulment, to speak to Josh and lay some ghosts to rest. She accepted his apology. To avoid becoming a bitter old battle-axe, she realised the same action was necessary now.

'You're a mad hatter,' Titty instigated the exchange, 'but my world is a boring place without your harebrained ideas.'

'And your experience of Glastonbury is oh-so-upper-class staying in the local 5-star hotel while the rest of us slum it in tents,' she replied, 'but I've missed you, too.'

The trio hugged.

'It's stopped raining,' Chloe ran into the cubicle in a tea dress and Doc Martens splashed with mud.

Sure enough, the torrents of water pummelling the tee-pee roof eased to the drip-drip of a leaky gutter.

'I didn't realise your mother approved of music festivals?' Titty remarked.

'Ssh,' Chloe raised a finger to her electric purple lips, 'it's our little secret.'

'While Horatia's away,' Charlotte joked, referencing the financier's business trip to Hong Kong, 'Chloe and I can play. We're having a whale of a summer together. It was definitely a white lie worth telling.'

After the phantom pregnancy was exposed, Horatia had considered their battle won – financier defeats wall flower – but she had underestimated Charlotte's bond with Chloe.

The women smiled, watching the little girl try on Zoë's round sunglasses like Yoko Ono circa 1976 and raid her woven bag for glitter to dab along her cheekbones.

'Any progress with John?' Titty asked.

'Slowly, but surely. Horatia felt sidelined by the baby so she dumped him. We're co-habiting again as friends not lovers. But he's crept into my bed on a few occasions.'

Zoë gave a toothy grin, then she looked to the women on her right.

'Josh really does love you.'

'Don't be fooled,' Titty disparaged the footballer who'd decayed her morals. 'Cheaters can't alter their DNA. Everything he says is claptrap. He's probably uses that line on all the girls.'

'Not true,' she corrected.

'How do you know?'

'Because he never used it on me.'

'What?'

'In our 12-month relationship, Josh never told me he loved me. He always glossed over the question. I ignored it, pretended his caginess was normal for men, but it shows he wouldn't use those words unless he meant them.'

'Titty,' Charlotte smiled, 'for the first time in your life, let someone love you for who you really are.'

A nurse interrupted their reunion.

'Dr Wedgewood-Beaverbrook, there's a backlog of patients waiting for a consultation,' she tutted.

'Of course.'

'Ah, before I forget, which one of you is Zoë Hornby?'

'Me, with the broken big toe.'

'Dr Kent asked me to give you his number.'

'Why?' Zoë was confused.

'Apparently, he's available should you require any "after-care".'

'See, girls,' she winked, excited by the salary of a top-notch doctor, 'I suppose it's true what people say. Cupid works in mysterious ways.'

Printed in Great Britain
by Amazon